Alex Van Halen

Biography

A Lifetime of Rock and Roll

CONTENT

Chapter 1

Music is where our story begins, no matter how you start it. Even if you started before we were born. Our father, Jan Van Halen, was a Dutch musician who had performed in orchestras and jazz groups around Europe. When World War II broke out, he joined the Dutch air force, where he played in the marching band. He was rightfully proud of that. He never mentioned what happened next: the Germans invaded Holland in 1940, conscripting the whole Dutch army. If you refused, you were shot dead on the spot. So the next thing he knows, my father is being forced to play German oompah music and propaganda songs, essentially with a gun to his head.

When I was born on May 8, 1953, and Ed joined the party twenty months later, my mother was anxious to make us respectable in ways her husband was not. Her plan included classical music, which is why my brother's name is Edward Lodewijk Van Halen. (That is Dutch for Ludwig, as in Beethoven—whose real surname was van Beethoven, by the way.) We had a Rippen upright piano, and Mom had us take lessons. We weren't permitted to leave the house unless we'd practised, which became a source of contention. Ed and I were both good at it, and my mother was very proud of our abilities and had high expectations for us. She wished for us to be well-educated and white-collar someday, imagining concert pianists performing at Carnegie Hall rather than Van Halen and the Monsters of Rock.

We resided in a flat in a block of six apartment buildings, with one of my mother's sisters living next door. That was our world—the flats, the church, and the school. The rest did not exist. The flat was always frigid, with the main source of heat being a small hot water boiler in the kitchen. When I was a newborn, my mother put me in my bassinet directly next to it to keep me warm before leaving to do something else. When she came back in, I had turned blue. The pilot light had burned out, and I'd been gassed. I definitely lost half my brain cells that morning and have been seeking them ever since. My parents were traditional and old-school. They did not treat us as babies. Dad had a footlocker where he stored his air force uniform and a 25-clip submachine pistol. We played with both. Fiddling with that rifle is one of my earliest memories; I was maybe five or six years old.

In Holland, the guys we knew worked and drank. Other musicians, as well as my father's two brothers and their wives, would visit our flat on occasion, and things would get wild. My father was a sweet, delicate, soft-spoken man until he drank. Then he became the life of the party. My mother, on the other hand, never consumed alcohol. When he returned home from a hard day—or night—of work, wanted to unwind, and had a few too many, she would stare at him: why don't you do this or that, wear a suit, and be an upstanding member of society? That is all she wanted. Three of my mother's sisters had migrated to Holland, and I believe there was always some competition about who married best. My aunt Deedee in the flat next door believed she was the big cheese since her husband was a Coca-Cola executive who was constantly bringing home bottles of the beverage. My cousins soon developed decaying Coca-Cola teeth.

If you start our story in 1962 with a two-week boat voyage from Holland to America, you'll probably guess what I remember: music. I was eight years old, and Ed was six, when our father arranged for us to work. We were the freak show piano-playing small kids who got to sit at the captain's table after our performance, which my father had arranged as recompense. My attitude was, "I am taking over here." (I was overconfident as a kid... and possibly as a young man.) We'd been in the boat's bowels, in third class, and two days later we were up first, sitting with the captain, making it our usual hangout. It was simply our tendency to hunt for an angle in whatever we did.

When we arrived in New York, they discovered that our piano had somehow gotten misplaced in the freight hold. My father suggested,

"Let's just stay here, we can live in New York." But my mother was determined: we had a sponsor and a place to stay in Pasadena, and oranges cost a cent each. She was from the tropics, and those oranges loomed enormous.

So we rode a train across the nation. It was dubbed the Dreamliner, and the car in the middle featured a large skylight—"the Great Dome," through which you could see the trees and houses passing by. I recallEd telling myself, "You missed the Indians, man!" after I awoke from my nap. Apparently, when we arrived in Phoenix or some other western town, they had individuals dressed in feathers climb on top of the train. (It was a different time.) I couldn't believe Ed hadn't awakened me up for this. I was definitely upset at him the entire way through Nevada.

It was a four-day journey, and the main topic of conversation for the majority of it was whether we should stop in Chicago. My father supported it, but my mother insisted: "No, no, no, we're going to LA because that's where my family is." When we arrived, we were still wearing our big-ass winter coats from Holland, and it was scorching hot. My uncle picked us up in a baby-blue '56 Ford convertible. Ed and I were looking at the car, thinking, "We've arrived!" That type of vehicle is not available in Holland. That type of weather is not common in Holland. Northern Europe is constantly and viciously grey. In Southern California, everything was bright as hell. It was stunning and overwhelming, as if we'd arrived in a completely different universe—like Dorothy waking up in Oz rather than Kansas, taking in the Technicolor. I thought, "This is the shit." I'll never leave. And I never have.

American culture was mind-bending and immensely fascinating. We could not believe the cartoons! In Holland, you could only watch TV for around twenty minutes once a week. In California, it appeared that Felix the Cat was always on black-and-white television. We couldn't get enough of it, which was fortunate since while everyone else was at work—or, in my parents' case, looking for it—Ed and I were alone with the cartoons. They'd leave at 7 a.m. and tell us, "Just keep the TV on this channel and we'll see you at four." Okay. We can do it. We had no idea where he was at first, and even when we learned he was in jail, we didn't realise someone was supposed to go and bail him out. That's not how things work in Holland, where we were familiar with the system. My father had been tossed in the can on occasion for drunken and rowdy behaviour. No one in the family explained bail to us in California. (Don't forget, my mother had married a white man. After fifteen days, we figured it out and went to get my father. If my mother was annoyed with her sister for being less than forthright, she kept it hidden. The truth was that it was my aunt's encouragement that brought us to California, and she had two sons who were roughly the same age as me and Ed. But we never played much, and after the first month or two, we went our separate ways. If you start our story with Ed and me as two young Dutch kids who didn't speak English and had to figure out how to fit into primary school in Pasadena, our new home, you'll see that we did so through music. One of the first things I remember about our new school, McKinley Elementary, was that all of the Black students—perhaps thirty—were in the same class. I couldn't figure out why that was. I did not inquire, however. At that age, you assume that everything you see is exactly how it is. Plus, we had just arrived in a foreign nation, and I had no idea what the restrictions were. Pasadena's rules in the early 1960s remained de facto segregation.

Fortunately for us, European schools were far more advanced than those in the United States, so we began with an academic advantage. (And I was exaggerating; we only knew one English word: "accident." It was the first word in the alphabetized "how to learn English" book that my mother had taken on the boat. Ed and I were both athletic, which gave us another advantage. Baseball and basketball—as you might expect, Ed had incredible hand-eye coordination; he was second to none. However, he was also quite fast and excelled in track and field. His finest event was the fifty-yard dash sprint. I was the miller, the long-distance runner. (Representing our distinct personalities: I'm the rock, he's the roll. Ed could not sit still. He was constantly wolfing down breakfast, for example. What's the hurry? We have a long day ahead of us. Let's not waste all of our energy before we leave the house! We eventually became "squad leaders," which simply meant you could wear a red bandana around your waist and command everyone what to do. But that happened later. When we initially arrived in America, music helped us adjust to our new surroundings.

After my parents were able to get us our own house, Ed and I became friends with two boys who lived up the block, Brian and Kevin. Everywhere we went, we made friends with brothers: Greg and David, Ross and Bill, Brian and Kevin. They arrived in pairs. Ed would befriend the younger, while I would befriend the older. Brian and Kevin had no musical experience, but they did have a plastic Emenee guitar, which drew us in. We'd been playing drums on empty Baskin-Robbins ice cream containers and a guitar made of a shoebox with a paper towel roll taped to its ass. A plastic toy represented a step up. Even better, Brian and Kevin had an older brother who had an actual drum kit, which we occasionally used. Our mother may have forced us to study the piano, but our father taught us about musicianship by example. I recall sitting in the room with him, watching him build his own reeds. He would shave them with a plane and then smooth them with sandpaper to achieve the desired tone, feel, and fit for his mouthpiece. Then he'd sit in a room for an hour, playing the same note until it was perfect. Humidity, temperature, and other environmental factors can have an impact on woodwind instruments. Most clarinet players have a very glassy sound, but our father had a woody sound—a richer, earthier tone— and it wasn't by mistake. (This later influenced what Ed and I referred to as the "brown sound" that we were looking for.) My father would sit there, completely absorbed in whatever he was doing. His entire world became a reed in his mouth.

Ed and I took first place in our respective age groups at the Long Beach City College classical piano contest three years in a row outperforming thousands of other young competitors. Our teacher was a bright man who had studied at the Imperial Conservatory in Saint Petersburg, Russia, and he used to hit our hands with his ruler when we made mistakes. He didn't find out about my inability to read until much later, when he was playing a new piece of music and asked me to flip the page. He discovered it after roughly five years of classes with the guy, which made him unhappy. It was cramped at our apartment. I can see every inch of it. You had the piano and the television in the living room, followed by my drum kit and Ed's amplifiers years later. Eventually, there was this enormous organ with a rhythm box that my mother would play on holidays, pounding out the oldies with my father joining her on sax. The kitchen was next, followed by Ed's "bedroom," which was actually simply a foyer leading to the back door. He had no privacy—if you wanted to enter or exit our house, you went through Ed's room. The next door was our parents' bedroom, and if you walked a little further, you'd arrive at my space: an add-on to the house constructed of plywood so thin it was more like cardboard; you could put your foot through it without even trying. It was on a concrete slab, and there was no heat. Both Ed's and my rooms had unique disadvantages—I got to choose mine first since I was older, and I wanted one that was far enough away from everyone that I could have some alone time every now and then.

My father used to practise with his band in our house, and I would pick up their instruments while they were taking breaks. I learnt to play the saxophone this way. My father's band's drummer was a guy named Max—a typical drummer with a twinkle in his eye and everything done with a little levity. I suppose he recognized that I enjoyed what he was doing. He gave me my first drum: a marching snare. He showed me the ropes. One day, he taught me something called pannenkoeken, which is simply Dutch for "pancakes": a double-stroke roll. And I'm watching him as he goes into this buzz roll, and it's incredible how he does it. My father would occasionally take us with him to his engagements. It was my first exposure to the environment of a dark club—very sexual, extremely alluring. The women are wearing a lot of perfume, and I can tell by the way they dance. It's not a mystery why you're all there. Even a child can figure that out. The music serves as the background for the evening's romance. And I was pulled to that from a young age. When I was eleven, I had my first romantic contact with an older woman onstage. (Remember, when you're eleven, everyone is older.) There was so much excitement and carousing; it just sort of occurred. It was over sixty years ago, so I don't recall much... It's like a hazy memory of a doctor's visit. A most pleasant one.

My father used to remark that a musician can perform on anything, including a chair. It is about expressing a sentiment. "It was my mom who really cracked the whip and wanted us to be proper musicians; she didn't want us to struggle playing nightclubs like our dad," Ed once told guitar journalists Brad Tolinski and Chris Gill. My mother got us into violin next, when I was in fourth grade and Ed was in second, and that became the source of fistfights: guys wandering around with little violin cases just as well have been wearing targets. (We gave as good as we received). Ed and I practised violin for roughly five years before joining the All City Orchestra, which includes Pasadena's top young performers. That meant taking the bus after school every day to rehearse. The first of many bus trips to come.

I remember going to Local 47, the musicians' union, with my father when I was maybe ten and Ed was eight, and seeing all these tremendously gifted guys being treated like dog meat. They were all dressed in worn-out, ill-fitting clothes that they'd been sitting in for far too long, leaving their rears glossy and ragged. (Because we were short, our eyes were almost at eye level, so we had plenty of time to think about those trousers while we waited in line.) I remember the stench of stale cigarette smoke. That, and looked at Ed and said, "We're not going to end up here. "This is nonsense." We learnt to set our goals higher, on things that might or might not work out, but we weren't going to give up. A few years later, when I was thirteen, I had my first professional job. It was New Year's Eve—a huge night for a band like my father's—and their drummer, Max, had a high-paying performance scheduled. When the band was offered a last-minute gig at the Continental, a bar near the Continental bus stop on Cahuenga Boulevard, my father responded, "You're coming along."

I never doubted that I'd be in a band, especially with my brother. However, we had no idea what kind of music we would perform until the British Invasion made it plain. We were enthralled by the wildness and rebellion of rock. What's with the rock 'n' roll being bigger than life? That certainly appealed to us. It made me feel hopeful. There was a sense of drifting gloom at the time, and we didn't have a positive outlook on the future. The Cuban Missile Crisis occurred months after we docked in New York! We were certain we were going to be bombed. Rock 'n' roll made you want to dance, twist, and holler. It made you feel better—and that's what people remember about a band: how they felt, not what they played.

For a while, Ed and I went door to door with a can of spray paint and a stencil, offering to repaint people's street numbers on the curb for a small charge. Ed eventually acquired his drums and I got my guitar, thanks to some money and a loan from our father. The goal was to form a band; I don't think one of us was particularly dedicated to any one instrument at the time. Ed didn't mind if I played around on his drum set, and I was content to let him strum my Teisco.

Chapter 2

We used to have a toy gun, a small Mattel shotgun. Ed and I got into a fight one day about whose turn it was to play with the item. My father steps forward, grabs the gun, and breaks it in half. He says, "Here." Now you all have a slice." It broke my heart. But it taught me that 100% of nothing is nothing. My father, King Solomon of Pasadena, was extraordinary in the manner he taught us. It was just small nuggets here and there, and after a few years, you'd understand, "Oh, that's what he meant." The most essential lesson he taught us—with that gun and in a hundred other ways—was to keep together.

I'VE BEEN SOBER FOR DECADES, but if memory serves, part of the fascination of wine is that you're drinking something that's both alive—grape juice fermenting—and on its road to death: ultimately, the stuff will cease ripening to perfection and simply go off. So, in a way, you're drinking the life cycle. And the slight flavour of decay can be quite alluring. Along the same lines, Ed's greatness was more than just the way he played a note. The enchantment was also in the way he'd cause the sounds to fade, or die. Next time you listen to him, pay attention: the noises going are just as interesting as the sounds coming. I realise this sounds like a reach, but I believe Ed was able to transmit significant truths about the universe through his music.

One of Ed's favourite aspects of guitar was that he suddenly had more control over his sound—he could express himself in more nuanced ways since he was in charge of the strings themselves. The strings were insufficient, of course. Ed eventually decided to mess with the entire guitar. After a few years with Teisco, he moved to a hollow-body Univox Custom twelve-string guitar with a gorgeous red-and-black sunburst finish. He decided he just wanted six strings, so he eliminated all of the upper-octave strings. "That was my very, very first successful attempt at changing something on a guitar that

11

was not up to my liking," he told me. It became a way of life.

He tried everything—stuffing the amp with padding, directing it toward the wall—to obtain the feedback tones he wanted without deafening everyone else. He eventually discovered that he could overload the vacuum tubes and generate those tones at a lower level by turning down the Variac variable power supply below 110 volts, which was a sort of solution. You have to understand that where we grew up, the idea of taking something you'd spent a lot of money on and modifying it to suit your own personal preferences did not seem weird. We were surrounded by hot rod culture; individuals were always souping up their vehicles with junkyard parts and modifying them with racing stripes, shiny hubcaps, and other accessories. We loved vehicles, but music was our lifeblood. Ed was not going to waste his valuable time and money on whatever crappy car we were driving around. He used all of his intelligence and inventiveness to adjust his instruments, bringing them just a little closer to his fantasy.

Naturally, we gravitated toward other kids who were music-obsessed, and some of them were quite important in our lives. There was Dan Scruggs, who introduced us to the blues, then Eric Clapton when I was about thirteen. We formed a band called the Trojan Rubber Company with him and another child, Denis Travis. (I know, classy.) Denis's father was a preacher who was vehemently opposed to drugs, but where there's a will, there's a way: we'd create "nuclear tea" before heading over there. You collect as many tea bags as you can find and steep them for hours on end until the brew is virtually black, and man, that stuff gives you a rush when you drink it.

It seems silly, but we didn't think so at the time. Honestly, I still respect the impulse. You do everything you think is necessary to become a better version of yourself—deeper, more articulate, and more creative. Every artist, whether visual or musical, has an itch that can't be scratched to connect with some universal vibration. It's always just out of reach, just around the corner, and that's what keeps them going. If you feel that sipping the world's strongest cup of tea will put you in the mood to be your most creative and productive, then go put the kettle on.

We began performing music "professionally" when my father would drag us along to his shows, where we learnt how everything worked. He instructed me early on that I should play each night as if it were my last, knowing that I would probably be playing forever. As in, give them everything you have. Give it to them again tomorrow. That's what he taught us and how he survived on his own. However, being a musician, particularly a drummer, was beginning to permeate into my identity. The dancers in the clubs where my father performed were mostly regular individuals who enjoyed ballroom dancing. But there were also some semi-professionals, and seeing them taught you when to step it up as a drummer.

Ed undoubtedly felt weird performing with my father's band because the guitar sections were far more challenging than the drums. For me, the answer was simple: if you could swing, you could maintain. It didn't matter what music it was, how the setups worked, and so on. Keep time and swing with the band. (My father used to say, "If anyone asks what ' wing' is, they'll never get it." You cannot define it. But you'll recognize it when you feel it!) Drums aren't always easier to play; there's simply less to remember. To get through the night on some of those old favourites, a guitarist needs a chart to keep track of where all the chords are.

Chapter 3

When I was six years old, my father offered me my first drink schnapps. Instead of a pacifier, he handed me a tobacco pipe to calm me down. You must understand that in postwar Holland, everyone around us was smoking and drinking. In Northern Europe, alcohol is served during ceremonies, in churches, and at supper. You need alcohol to get through the winter—and the winter lasts forever.

We were taught that drinking was simply what you did: to celebrate to party, to relax, and to brace yourself for when things went wrong When Ed was twelve, my cousin's German shepherd leaped through the screen door and buried his teeth on my brother's thigh. My father's prescription was to give him a cigarette and a shot of vodka (Dogs despised Ed; they were continually pursuing him. Maybe it was because he emanated so much vulnerability, but who knows Whatever the reason, it occurred frequently. I recall once going over to see our friend Julio. We had just gone in, and I was gazing about when I heard yelling and screaming: Ed was being chased down the street by a beagle. The funniest thing I've ever seen.

Alcohol was clearly a problem in our household. I remember going to see my father after they had thrown him in a military hospital to dry out before we left Holland. I didn't grasp what was going on a the moment. All I knew was that it was your father; go visit him. remember the scent of ether and the fact that the institution was really low-tech—it looked like those photographs of Russian orphanages, with row after row of sterile cots. I pretended nothing was amiss or out of the ordinary. My mother didn't explain or say anything about where we were or what we were doing, so I spent the entire time looking out the window, hoping he wasn't too sick. At the time, you didn't really question your parents. They knew everything and, most importantly, ruled everything, so you simply followed everything they said.

One of the things I learned growing up was that you really have to be able to pivot, you really have to be able to navigate, because at any one time, maybe your dad is right—but now maybe your mom is right—and you're stuck in this crazy turmoil, and you have to adjust quickly. Things would worsen. My father was occasionally out of line. When you're a youngster, you simply do what your mother says. So I had to go ahead with it. I struck him on the head with a glass quart bottle of Miller beer.

We were a physical family. "I'm going to kick your ass" was almost a phrase of endearment with us. My father kept a blackjack beneath the stairs and was constantly threatening to beat us with it if we did this or that. He never did; the worst that could happen was he'd smack us if we got out of control. Ed and I played tough, as most brothers do. When my father wanted to sit down and have a nice meal after a hard day—which typically followed a long night—he would get annoyed with me and Ed causing havoc, laughing wildly, running around the table, and one of us would get slapped.

Ed and I, like all brothers, or at least the brothers I know, beat each other whenever we had the opportunity. I still have a scar on my face from when Ed cut me with a bamboo "sword" while we were in Holland. What occurred was that one morning, my mother had a cup of coffee, which she placed on the washing machine. Ed grabbed something, and his palm smacked the saucer, spilling boiling-hot coffee on him; he suffered second- and third-degree burns all over his body. My parents took him to the hospital, where they wrapped him in bandages like a mummy and deliberately put small bamboo sticks to keep the bandages from clinging to his blisters. It wasn't long before we started practising fencing with those bamboo sticks. There were very few things we did separately. The presumption was that whatever I did, he did, and vice versa, particularly when it came to music. Any deviation from this was uncomfortable.

Ed felt left out when I went to work with my father and he was not invited since he was still a child. Ed, being the second child, was always fighting for his father's attention. Of course, I was thinking, "Be my guest, Ed, and go do all this shit instead of me!" I wasn't sure if I wanted to work all the time at eleven or twelve years old. But to Ed, it appeared that we were doing something together that he was not involved in. I suppose that's how it is with siblings. Then there was a band that rehearsed in a washing machine business in Monrovia, and they went after Ed. We went to see them, and I must have been at least sixteen because I drove us there. Their enticement was that they had a record contract. And you remember—I do—my father saying, "Don't fight over the gun, so to speak." Once your foot is in the door, you can move about. If they have a record deal, this may be beneficial for us.

The first concert we ever saw was Clapton and Derek and the Dominos at the Pasadena Civic Auditorium in 1970. A friend of Ed's had won the tickets from a local radio station and given them to him because he knew Clapton was Ed's god. We were in the sixth row, but Ed brought binoculars to watch every detail of Clapton's performance.

"I HATED FOLLOWING YOU IN SCHOOL," Ed told me repeatedly. There were two issues: I got decent grades (at least when I tried), and I was a troublemaker.

In terms of the first, I began as a straight-A student. I believe it was a fluke occurrence, but they tested me, and I performed well. I wish they hadn't—it caused me nothing but anguish, and I doubt it means anything. But my mother did. She took that to heart, and the next thing you know, there was this little four-foot-tall Indonesian woman walking into the school, plainly out of place, antagonising all of the professors. She wanted me in the gifted program, but I didn't want to be there. Because I did not observe any attractive girls in the class! That demonstrates where my—supposedly intelligent—head was at.

16

I got into a physical fight with Mr. Carlson, my high school shop instructor. You see, we had an off-campus paper called the Bull Sheet, which contained everyone's thoughts on everything going on at school. You were not permitted to remain anonymous: if you want to say anything stupid, fine, but you must sign your name and accept responsibility. It was the second to final day of high school, and I had the Bull Sheet. Mr. Carlson approached me and said, "Give me that." I said, "No way." So he became pushy, and I pushed back. My impression was that there was no chance for me; I needed to go to Vietnam quickly. So I threw a swing at Mr. Carlson and wound up in the principal's office.

I accepted the deal. Mr. Charles did not specify that he would give me a D-minus average. But I got by, which was more than most of my pals could claim. Academically, Ed and my group had no direction; we were not there to gain an education. You knew you couldn't afford to attend college. And I'd already determined that if they summoned me to go to Vietnam, I'd go—this country welcomed us. It never occurred, however, since my draft number was too high. Ed got himself into trouble. He was dismissed from our educational system when he was sixteen or seventeen after being arrested for possession—of a joint, but that was sufficient. It was a felony charge, and we weren't citizens yet, so my parents were concerned that we might be deported. My father was as casual as usual: "Well, maybe we'll move to Scotland." I, on the other hand, went and beat up the guy who had ratted Ed out. The entire school witnessed me kick the ass of the boy who allegedly told Ed. The cops eventually came and arrested me, and I was sentenced to a couple of years on probation. But that's not the worst part. I banged up the wrong person.

I felt terrible about it—I knew it was wrong. Karma brought me back. A few months later, I was hanging out in the park when a gang of seven or eight guys approached and beat the living crap out of me with golf clubs. Ed witnessed the entire scene from a distance, but he had no idea I was at the bottom of the pile. These were individuals who had nothing to do with the poor schmuck at school I'd pummelling—there was no connection between the two beatings, except in my head, where it appeared that I had received what I deserved. Ed ended up having to go to a place called continuing education, where you won't learn anything but how to keep doing what brought you there in the first place. He was always rebellious, which is why rock 'n' roll appealed to him.

You can imagine how disappointed my mother was, as she had hoped to raise two respectable young men. She'd rant and scream at us, or simply shake her head. Ed and I naturally gravitated toward the outcasts—we weren't among the tennis racket-wielding set. Pasadena was not always the homogeneous, manicured suburb it is now. We come from a mixed neighbourhood with Native American, Hispanic, and Black children, where people battled and the milieu was tough. The truth is that only one of the guys I hung out with in high school, aside from myself, has survived.

So I did. As a teenager, in addition to finishing high school, I was already taking extra classes at this electrician school and working two or three different jobs because we needed the money, plus I was trying to get the band started and needed some time for my newfound interests in drinking, drugs, and girls. I was stretched thin! There were so many conflicting demands and difficulties, and I felt like I was doing my part—pulling my weight and then some. Maybe that's why, one day, when I went home from school and my father came up behind me and smacked me over the head because he thought I was skipping class, I clocked him. It's definitely the most upsetting act I've done, and the one I'm most ashamed of. He falsely accused me of a minor infraction of our family's honour code, to which I retaliated with the most serious offence imaginable. We never discussed it during our entire time working together, driving to these gigs in the middle of nowhere. After that episode, my father and I didn't talk much for a year or two. We just had a drink together. Often, on those long rides home after playing music at a club, we were both as drunk as skunks and couldn't see the road.

Chapter 4

I recall going to see Zeppelin with Ed at the Forum when I was about sixteen, and it was practically a holy experience for us. The scent of marijuana was so strong in there that we thought we were inside a bong. And the sound was simply fantastic. The drawback was that they didn't play anything exactly as it was on the record, but rather the sheer, raw nakedness of it, the wall of sound coming at us. It was utterly overwhelming. Those guys could have played "Happy Birthday" and it would have turned into a rock 'n' roll song—they were so unique! And it was amazing to be surrounded by so many other young people who adored them (nearly) as much as we did. And who just wanted to blast the roof off.

We wanted to enter a highly lively, fertile music environment because of the energy, vibe, and not just the sound. Everyone had their own distinct style, from Zeppelin and the Beatles to T. Rex and the Doobie Brothers. When my father returned home from work on weekends, we would gather around the TV to watch Don Kirshner's Rock Concert or The Midnight Special. He'd give a brief running commentary on easy topics. When we were watching Liberace, my father said, "You see the candelabra?" That was all he said. But I understood what he meant: What is your visual reference that distinguishes you from everyone else? Ed and I were simply two teenagers with long hair, dressed in T-shirts and corduroys. There was room to improve.

ED AND I DECIDED THAT no real band could exist without a manager, so we sought the assistance of a loudmouthed punk youngster, who booked up a concert for us at what has since become a notorious party in a Pasadena park. Ed and I arrive first—as we always do—to assess the situation, check the power supply, and see how the lighting is. There was nothing to see: no stage or lighting. Nothing. A few hours later, we returned to the park. Another local band, Red Ball Jet, was performing. They were dreadful, at least to our way of thinking. The music was really unremarkable. Anyway, one thing led to another, and I'm not sure why I tossed a bottle at them. Not to damage anyone, but to say, Hey, we'll take some of that attention over here! That kind of paused the music, and Ed and I made our way up there to say hello to the Komora brothers, Miles and Mark, who played bass and guitar in that band that we knew from around town. We just wanted to know how the hell they ended up playing a gig we had scheduled. They were quite lovely people. But anyway, people started pushing and shoving, and before you knew it, the texture, colour, and flavour of the entire thing had become horrible. Someone pulled a knife. A mini-riot broke out.

That was my first time with Red Ball Jet and their lead singer, Dave Roth.

In my imagination, I was about sixteen when I hurled that bottle, and years passed until Dave auditioned for Ed and me. But the chronology does not add up. Time moves differently when you're a teenager, extending out over the tedium of high school. It couldn't have been more than a few months. What I do know is that Dave was constantly on the fringe of our vision from that point forward. We'd run into him at the temple—we were playing, Dave was praying, as I always said, because Dave is Jewish. The temple was a cultural nexus in our neighbourhood, and they graciously allowed us to rehearse there, so we'd play at their dances and meet Dave there, as well as at backyard parties throughout Pasadena. Dave would see us.

Dave was a hyperactive child who had been in leg braces since he was four years old. I'm not sure what they were mending, but they must have done something well because by the time we got our hands on him, he was able to use those legs on stage. He'd always yearned for an audience. Dave had already moved around the country when we met him. He was born in Bloomington, Indiana, where his father attended medical school to become an ophthalmologist. Dr. Roth graduated, and they spent some time on a horse ranch in the Midwest. (I own one today because my wife, Stine, competes in dressage across the country. I don't ride horses, but I do enjoy being around them and spending time at the ranch, which is serene and bucolic. I get the appeal. Dave and his sisters, Allison and Lisa, relocated with their parents to Brookline, Massachusetts, a posh suburb of Boston, before making the final trek west to California.

It didn't go well. We agreed to play Johnny Winter's song "Still Alive and Well." But Dave couldn't get the lyrics out on the beat, so Ed and I finished playing before he could start singing. I'm exaggerating, but only slightly: timing was not his strong suit. "He could not sing." We were young and rigid, so we told Dave, "Thanks but no thanks; it wasn't a good fit." It was all extremely courteous and professional, and we got along well with the Komora brothers at Pasadena backyard gatherings.

We said yes to every possible gig. We were always playing. First and foremost, it was all we wanted to achieve, and secondly, keep in mind that Steve Winwood was only sixteen when he issued his debut song. Ed and I were lagging behind. We changed our name from the Broken Combs to Genesis, which we believed sounded more mature and professional. Unfortunately, we discovered that there was already a British band with that name, and they were far further advanced than we were, having previously released an album. We chose to call ourselves Mammoth instead, because that was how huge we were going to be.

He had no sense of timing when singing, but he did have an unusual drawl. He was very unfamiliar with our type of music. He adored Louis Prima. He really wanted to be Al Jolson or James Brown. "The first records that I imitated were Al Jolson—getting down on one knee, you know, with the white gloves, singing, as well as dancing— the idea of entertaining," Dave says. "Jolson was the first one to really construct a whole show with a wardrobe, dancers, his own lights, his own sound, his own orchestra, and take it on the road." Dave's natural passion with showmanship, his drive to draw as much attention to himself as possible, was everything we lacked.

We knew enough to realise that a guy like Dave, with his ego and charisma, would allow us to be more authentic. The crowd could watch Dave while we played. He knew that was his role, and he enjoyed it. Years later, he summarised his contribution to Van Halen as follows: "I look forward to making a show." It's showbiz, Broadway, tinsel, glitter town, Hollywood, the lines, Auntie Mame, and Bali Ha'i is calling! Boom." Yeah. That wasn't what Ed and I brought to the table.

On the one hand, I thought his musical taste was a little strange. But then I realised that combining our and his ideas would result in something completely unique... a soup with an intriguing blend of ingredients and layers of flavours that might taste unlike anything you'd ever had before. Plus, Dave shared our determination and work ethic, which is incredibly unique. And he had the PA system.

Dave persuaded me he should join the band, and I persuaded Ed. Without my encouragement, Ed would never have met Dave. I was the older brother, and I was the one who persuaded him that this was what we needed to do. So this is my fault! I believed that if Dave could get me to join the band, he could persuade anyone else. Who will win if there are five candidates vying for a single seat? The loudest, obnoxious, and violent motherfucker on the globe. Dave, you got the job!

We've always had day jobs. Following his paper route, Ed began moving pianos and organs for Berry & Grassmueck, a music store in Pasadena. That's when he came across a Marshall stack—a hundred-watt amplifier head and two speaker cabinets—that had been used as the house amp at the Rose Palace, a massive cement facility in

Pasadena where they assembled floats for the Rose Parade and occasionally held concerts. Jimi Hendrix performed there—through that amplifier. In general, Marshalls were difficult to get by, and they were the chosen amplifiers of Ed's favourite guitar players: Clapton utilised a Marshall, as did Jimmy Page. "I had never seen a Marshall before except in pictures," Ed informed me. "I told them I didn't care how long I had to work there; I just wanted that amp. I only cared that it was Marshall." Ed purchased it using his employment discount and spent years moving pianos to pay it off.

I started working at a machine shop the day after I graduated from high school; it was as if I had walked right out of school. Every malcontent and pervert you can think of worked beside me, as did some really hard working immigrant family guys. I had a great time for a while, but I nearly lost a finger. I worked in the milling department, where I had the largest machine (of course). One day, while fiddling around with this big magnetic plate, it flies away. My finger goes through the machine and then hangs from a thread. They hurried me to the hospital and stitched me back together. That finger still feels strangely numb; it's an odd sensation. (It accounts for the distinct snare sound I receive. That finger is like a deadweight, acting as a damper, killing the overtones). The machine did not chop through the bone because I was hit with a grinding stone rather than a blade. If it had been a blade, my life would have been very different.

After leaving the machine shop, I bought my first decent drum equipment. It was a Ludwig, and it cost one thousand dollars. I recall walking inside the Village Music Store in Sierra Madre. Mr. Shepherd, the proprietor, was a wonderfully lovely guy, and I paid him with the one-dollar bills I had made at the business. That mound of cash represented a thousand hours of my effort, a thousand hours of my life, and he knew it. I still have the drum equipment. We've enjoyed some great times together.

Dave had a friend, Liz, who told us we could rehearse in her garage for free! It was incredibly gracious of her, and we were grateful for the room; I taught her young boy how to play drums. The only issue was that her house was in a bad neighbourhood, so we had to take down all of our equipment every night when we finished and then bring it back to set up the next day; if we had left it overnight, it would have been stolen. We had a keyboard player in the band for a short time, primarily because he brought with him a dance studio that his family owned and enabled us to use for rehearsal. He had amazing pitch but lacked common sense! Eventually, we had to separate ways.

We ended up rehearsing in Dave's basement, which I considered a poor idea. He has the authority now; you are not going to tell him, "This isn't working, man," after his family has gone out of their way to let us play there. Not that the location was ideal: after a hard rain, the basement would leak a little, forcing us to rush over there and stack all of the equipment on pallets. We weren't going to complain because it was rent-free. And nobody could hear us down there, which was amazing. The key point is that we had nothing, and anything is preferable to nothing.

Dave grew up with show-tune-loving parents, and his father's brother, Uncle Manny, gave him his first radio—Uncle Manny was a significant influence. In the early 1960s, he launched Café Wha?, a well-known coffeehouse in Greenwich Village. ("Manny came up with the name while walking from couch to couch one night, asking, 'What shall we name our new coffeehouse?'" And someone might suggest, 'How about "the Ever-Arcing Spiral of Transcendence"?' According to Dave, Manny would say, 'Wha?' like Grandma would. "So eventually he named it Café Wha?") There were performances by Lenny Bruce, Bob Dylan, Joan Rivers, and Allen Ginsberg, among others. Dave spent his vacations in New York City soaking up all of the strangeness and variety of the culture.

The first song we played after Dave joined the band was "It's You
Thing" by the Isley Brothers, because that was what he wanted to do
It was not Zeppelin. It wasn't deep purple. It wasn't like anything
we'd grown up with. Dave was clearly from a different planet—o
musical dimension—than we were. "When I first joined the band,
tried to sing some of their songs, including Grand Funk Railroad an
Black Sabbath. The song was quite unfamiliar to me. "I didn't own
those records," Dave acknowledges. True enough. However, we
considered adaptability as an important aspect of professionalism: we
can play anything. So we performed "It's Your Thing." We never
received any work after auditioning with the song, though. So you
start tinkering and adjusting. I forgot who said it (probably my
father), but if you play a song for the audience and they don't dance
don't play it again! Simple.

Look, I thought Dave was an oddball. But what impressed me was
that he was willing to do the work in the same way that we were. He
recognized the pattern: audition, play, practice, audition, play
practice. Go, go, go, 24 hours a day. I don't think people understand
that in order to be successful as a band, you have to work your ass to
the bone; it's not just about partying and getting girlfriends. (It was
not lost on me, however, that Ringo had all the chicks and was a
drummer with a large nose. Check, check. (If he can do it, so can I.)

We had more issues with our name. A cease-and-desist letter arrived
from another band, Mammoth. Ed and I considered changing our
name to Rat Salad. (It is the title of a Black Sabbath song from their
album Paranoid. But that's not an excuse. It was Dave's idea to
change our name to Van Halen. "To anyone who knows him and his
outsize ego, this would seem to be an uncharacteristically gracious
suggestion," our future manager Noel Monk has written regarding
Dave's planned name change, "but I don't think so. When it came to
job goals, David was nothing if not practical. He wanted nothing less
than to be famous, and he understood exactly how to get there."

Dave studied The Art of War and knew that if you offer someone anything, they will reciprocate. This will make it easy for you to do what you want. From the start, Dave understood he needed this band to get where he wanted to go.

THE FOUR YEARS BETWEEN FOURTEEN AND EIGHTEEN are a period of expansion and growth that is more intensive than the next twenty years combined. You go through a lot of changes, trying to figure out what you want. What are you planning to do? How? And how do you discover the perfect folks to bike with? Most folks do not. They do not devote the necessary time. Or their parents don't believe they can accomplish it. This is how we lost our first bassist, Mark Stone. So, we have our first real bass player. Before him, there was Mike Paloma. Then there was Frank—his girlfriend became pregnant, and that was it for him. He engaged us to play his wedding alongside his substitute, Kevin. Kevin was black, and they tried to turn us away at the wedding venue. I took out the contract and informed them that either they let us play the gig or I would sue them. They let us play. Kevin was a monster bass player, but he was also a monster marijuana user. He was eventually succeeded by Dennis. All of this happened before I was sixteen, when we met Mark Stone.

We thought he was wonderful, and it appears that he felt the same way. "I knew early on that they were both virtuosos," Mark stated in a 2003 documentary on Van Halen. "There were few legendary guitar players and I knew Edward was on his way to being there," he explained. "Alex was the leader. He was like the band's driving force, providing direction." Mark created the original Van Halen logo, with the V and A ending in small balls that resemble music notes. He was a very lovely, laid-back man. But Ed, Dave, and I had a different approach to our careers: we were all in. Mark was torn. "I was a straight-A student in school, and doing the band, and I was split between these two things," Mark said in the paper, "and basically I just couldn't keep up with them." I went to see his widow when he died—only ten days after Ed, if you can believe it. (See you on the other side, Mark). We will jam. They resided in the house where Mark had grown up. He bought it from his parents and stayed there indefinitely. She informed me that Mark had always felt that he had squandered a good opportunity.

Chapter 5

Dave, Ed, and I were always together from that point forward. We drove to the gigs together. We performed the gigs together. We rehearsed together. We ate together. God knows we drank together. We spent numerous hours in the middle of the night exploring Pasadena and the surrounding region for floodlights to steal off the outsides of apartment complexes and utilise for our presentations. Saying we were close misses the point: we were one.

I couldn't smoke weed with Dave like Ed could—that was their shared interest—because I couldn't play if I was stoned. (Believe me, if marijuana had been good for my creativity or helped me as a drummer, I would have become a regular Rastafarian.) Dave and I, however, had an interest in martial arts. When I was in high school, I went to International Karate on Colorado Boulevard and took instruction from this man named Henry. Some of the other guys in my class were real Paul Bunyan types, and their karate chops left welts on my arms. That won't assist my drumming. I stopped when Henry pushed another student through a wall, resulting in a collapsed sternum. More recently, I trained with this guy who serves as my Sicilian spiritual adviser. He keeps me disciplined and maintains the body functioning after seventy years of usage and abuse.

I didn't want to sing, let alone harmonise; I was too busy bashing on the drums. But once we had that certain combination of voices, things just started unfolding. Especially when we had to perform Top 40 covers in clubs, that's what people wanted to get up and dance to, so it just naturally evolved. We all become better at it. We mimicked bands like Humble Pie, who had incredible, strong vocals and treated them like another instrument. That is obviously something the Beatles did as well. And Queen gave everyone licence to be a serious hard rock band while yet having these wonderful harmonies laced throughout their songs. So now we had Mikey, who resided in the next town, Arcadia. We were a group of four, just like Led Zeppelin. The original Van Halen lineup was prepared to take on the world.

To convince our mother that we were doing something legitimate, Ed and I both began attending music classes at Pasadena City College, where Mikey and Dave were also enrolled. I thought we should improve our arrangement skills, be able to notate, and have all of the other requirements of becoming a professional musician; I wanted us to be prepared. We studied with Truman Fisher, who also had a notable student named Frank Zappa. Dave never really got into school; I doubt he could sit still for that long. Ed and I also learned a lot when sitting in front of the tube. The Tonight Show band was great. I enjoy big band arrangements, and Doc Severinsen did an excellent job putting everything together, as did Tommy Newsom and Ed Shaughnessy.

Dave owned an Opel Kadett station wagon, and we'd climb in there with our stuff and play wherever it took us. Motorcycle bars. Bowling alleys. Hispanic automobile clubs. Backyard parties were frequently shut down by cops, with the largest gatherings involving roughly a thousand individuals. Roller rinks. Local establishments with names like Perkins Palace, Barnacle Bill's, and the Proud Bird. There was this location called the International Casino, where the ceiling was so low that you would knock your head if you rose up too quickly from the drum kit, and the "dressing room" was a urinal with a pipe that went into the ground but wasn't connected to anything. You had to be there early before it stank so horrible your eyes watered.

I recall one night at Walter Mitty's in a lower-income neighbourhood of Pomona, when the entire establishment emptied out while we were playing—someone had been knifed. We witnessed the poor guy's stomach spilling out. We had to perform there again the next night, and in our wonderful wisdom, we positioned the amps a few feet away from the wall so that if the crap hit the fan again, we could hide behind them. We had a repertoire of approximately three hundred tunes. We didn't have a rhythm guitarist, so Ed was forced to step in whenever there was a gap, which became his style. But each club had its own playlist, so we had to accommodate that. If you're in a Latino establishment, you have to play whatever gets them up and dancing—you're not there to argue with the crowd, nor are you there to convert them. You're there to ease them into your music, because most people don't remember what you performed. They recall the way you made them feel.

The beauty of rock 'n' roll is that it appeals to anybody. Nobody goes to a show thinking, "I hope no one shows up." You're there because you are proud of what you've created and want to share it with as many people as possible. Our father always told us that if you take sides on anything, you would lose half of your audience. That's why we were unwaveringly apolitical.

Remember that drum solos were the stuff back then. That was probably the highlight of the evening. It got old, and people don't want to hear drum solos any longer. However, at the time, the pressure was on. One of the scariest things my father ever told me was, "When the drums come in, the song goes to the next level." Here's what we knew from the beginning. We are not there to perform a song. We are there to provide the necessary energy to rejoice. We weren't being videotaped; you had to be present to have the experience with us. We are there to start something with the audience. Van Halen is there to bring the party.

Chapter 6

We realised we couldn't spend the rest of our lives playing Pasadena The Sunset Strip was only nineteen miles away, but it seemed like another cosmos. Beginning in the spring of 1974, those became our hunting grounds. The Whisky a Go Go (yep, that's how they spell it and the Roxy were popular venues, but we couldn't even get auditions. The club scene was highly segregated—if you didn't have a record deal, you couldn't perform here; you could only play there and so on. Or there were venues like the Troubadour, where you couldn't really be rock 'n' roll; instead, you had to be a singer songwriter or something gentler, like the Eagles. Then there was Gazzarri's. It was kind of down and filthy, with a sordid vibe.

We auditioned once or twice for the owner, Bill Gazzarri, and he was unimpressed—just staring at us in our T-shirts and jeans, chewing on his cigar and shaking his head. Look, we were eager to do everything to be acknowledged. But, ultimately, we made it to Gazzarri's by doing what we do best. Mr. Gazzarri's bookers witnessed us play at Pasadena City College. By that point, whenever we played anywhere in the neighbourhood, at least a thousand people would turn up, and we must have been smoking that night, because the bookers were quite impressed. They persuaded Mr. Gazzarri to allow us a few nights to demonstrate what we could achieve with a crowd.

It didn't go well. Ed had purchased a decrepit Econoline van, and we arrived around midday to conduct our sound check on the day of our first show. However, there is only so much you can do in an empty space; everything must be adjusted once the crowd arrives. So that's done, and it's one thirty. What now? I'd heard John Bonham Zeppelin's drummer, remark that even if you're worried before a show, you shouldn't start drinking because you'll be tired—or worse—by the time you get on stage. So, drinking was out. We spen the remainder of the day sitting in the vehicle, growing increasingly agitated and frightened by the minute. God knows why; I suppose we felt compelled to be close to our equipment.

We are talking about 1974. America has just come out of Vietnam and Watergate. There was a lot of crime and a deep recession, and you could feel it in a variety of ways. We saw that every time we glanced at the Hollywood sign, which was meant to be this famous symbol of glamour but was actually going to pieces. To Mr. Gazzarri's horror, only about four people showed up on the first night we performed—no one else was present. That's not going to fly. Club owners make their money by selling alcohol, so we quickly discovered that you have to get them dancing, since the more they dance, the more they drink. Four people having a good time can outdance and outdrink fourteen people who are simply sitting about acting like they're in a library.

The entire day was geared toward the night. The entire day was nothing. We awoke at night. We usually played three sets per night. It was exhausting; only very young individuals can function in that manner. And the night didn't end when we finished performing at one or two a.m.; it had only just begun. We were a bunch of lads roaming around Hollywood unsupervised! And all around us were some of the best music clubs in the world. The Strip was a rock 'n' roll playground.

Most importantly, we were all improving our skills as musicians and entertainers. What is the boundary between the stage and the audience? We made it disappear. We learnt how to interact with a large number of people on an emotional level—how to draw them in and make them feel like they were a part of our project. Indispensable. When you play with the same individuals often, you establish timing and phrasing within the band. That can only be obtained by hard work. It's similar to having a dancing partner: you become acclimated to each other. Ed would always tune his guitar a quarter step lower—between E and D sharp—to fit Dave's narrow range and make his voice sound its best. When you work together in this manner to showcase everyone's skills, you wind up becoming more than the sum of your parts. Which is quite impressive when one of the components is a virtuoso like my brother.

If you're not sure where the phrase "rock 'n' roll" came from, look it up. You're there to get folks in the mood and relieve them of their inhibitions. When word spreads that there's a band that's good at it—and they're playing five, six nights a week—people start showing up. More dancing bodies means more drinking, which equals more money. So Mr. Gazzarri's satisfaction with us grew over time. "The females would often ask me, 'Godfather, could you introduce me to Eddie?' Gazzarri reportedly informed a journalist that Eddie was the most popular, despite being the quietest. "He would be on the side of the stage, and every week that we played them here, there would be at least fifty girls who would come and pay and sit on Eddie's side all night long."

With some of Gazzarri's money, we rented session time at Cherokee Studios in Chatsworth. Some of the tracks on that 1974 recording don't sound like Van Halen, with Dave crooning and muttering, for example. But we also recorded early versions of "Take Your Whiskey Home" and "In a Simple Rhyme," both of which appeared on our third album and are, in my opinion, great Van Halen songs. We were already creating original music that reflected our overall goal as a band. The only issue was that we could not perform our songs at Gazzarri's. We had to keep producing covers of whatever was on the radio. (Not that everything was horrible. (We played the Kinks to the ground.) We weren't treated like musicians there; rather, like a four-headed human jukebox. "We were supposed to get people into the bar, not the band," my brother explained.

Bill Gazzarri was a nice guy, and I will always be grateful to him, but he is lying when he says he discovered us. He didn't even know our names. He assumed Dave was named "Van" Halen, like Van

Morrison. Weeks become months. Months stretched into several years. Do you recall how long a year was when you were younger? I was in my early twenties, but it seemed like life was passing me by. At the end of the day, we were still simply the house band at a bar, and that wasn't going to suffice. I didn't want to be fifty years old, smoking cigarettes in line at the Local 47 while wearing those shiny-ass jeans. And I was not going to let that happen to Ed, a talented musician.

Rodney Bingenheimer was the "Mayor of the Sunset Strip" before becoming the "Prince of Pop," the DJ who hosted the best-known radio show for twenty years. Mick Jagger, Alice Cooper, David Bowie, Debbie Harry, and Neil Young are all seen kissing his ass in a documentary titled after him. The person was connected. He moved to town in the mid-1960s and soon found himself living with Sonny and Cher, performing their publicity. For a while, he ran his own club on the Strip called the English Disco, which you may have heard of. It had shut down before we arrived, but he was still everywhere—this short little guy with a quiet voice and a mop of bangs, like a West Coast Andy Warhol. He looked so much like Davy Jones that when Rodney auditioned for the Monkees and did not get the job, they kept him on as a body double for Jones in their films.

Anyway, Rodney saw us perform at Gazzarri's one night in 1976 and knew exactly what he was looking at. "The crowd was absolutely wonderful. A lot of chicks; I always assumed that bands with a lot of girls going crazy would make it big," he remarked. We invited Rodney to witness our presentation at the Pasadena Civic Auditorium and hear some of our own work. "When I got there, they had something like two thousand kids in the place," Rodney told the Los Angeles Times a year later. "They had organised the show themselves. Amazing." Putting such shows together was a production, as he correctly points out. You had to pay for the lights and the security, and you had to patch it all together—it could feel like you're impersonating a real band, because you're coming up with all these weird, half-assed, Band-Aid solutions to problems you don't fully understand because you're not a promoter, designer, or engineer; you're a MUSICIAN!

Rodney once brought Gene Simmons of Kiss to Starwood to check us out. We were fine that night. We were playing for a band named the Boyz, and their guitarist George Lynch once stated, "All I cared about was that they didn't suck and drive people away before our set." Then to witness everything you thought you understood about guitar playing shift right in front of your eyes during your own show? "Talk about depression!" Ed had that effect on his fellow guitarists: when they learned someone could play like my brother, they were torn between excitement and suicidal ideation.

We had a terrific time with Gene—I remember him taking us shopping for leather pants, which he suggested we needed if we wanted to be rock stars. (Look who you're asking: image Kiss sans the black leather. (You cannot.) The primary event was a recording session at Electric Lady, Jimi Hendrix's studio created in 1968 in the heart of Greenwich Village. We recorded fifteen songs, including "Runnin' With The Devil," "On Fire," and "House of Pain." However, none of it sounded good: the recording was terrible, and our performance was far from satisfactory. "I learned that I didn't like overdubbing," Ed stated of the incident. "Gene assumed I knew how it was done, but I said, 'Oh no, I can't do that.'" I wanted to continue to my usual style of playing, noodle in between chord lines. Instead, I had to fill in those gaps on the tape after recording the rhythm section, which was somewhat painful."

Gene took us to meet Kiss's manager, Bill Aucoin, and performed our demo for him. I'll never forget this: when we go to his office, he puts his feet up on the desk and has his shoes shined. We couldn't believe how irritating it was. He passed on us, but I believe we would have passed on him if given the opportunity. We were equally unimpressed with him as he was with us. Gene is a wonderful man, and I adore him. I will always be grateful for his early enthusiasm for us and comprehension of what we were doing. He's even been modest about it: "I was just honoured and lucky enough to be there to witness the greatness before it exploded on the world," he remarked. "This whole concept of 'you discovered Van Halen,' the ones who truly discovered the Van Halen brothers were their mother and father. After that, the two brothers created themselves. Nobody gave them anything. They worked hard for it. They put in the years. Thank you, Gene. Yes, we did.

When we returned home, Rodney Bingenheimer performed several of our demo tracks on his show Rodney on the ROQ, which aired on Pasadena radio station KROQ. However, we were still dissatisfied that nothing more had come of the situation. We believed it would be our big break, and we'd get signed and take over the world. "The world's most expensive demo tape," my brother once labelled our Gene Simmons recording in Guitar World. "We weren't sure where to take it. We didn't feel like going around to people's doors and saying, 'Sign us, sign us.' We just kept playing around till they came to us."

WHAT WE DID NOT KNOW AT THE TIME was that the club days were, in some ways, the peak of our experience on Earth. That was when we had the greatest highs, because the potential to be great was still there! That's when Van Halen's dream became the most magical—because it was still a dream. There is nothing more thrilling than believing you are on the edge of accomplishing all you have ever desired. This includes achieving it. A journalist once asked Ed if he missed anything from our club days. This was decades later, after we'd achieved many platinum records, toured the world, and made real money. "I miss how things back then were unknown," recalled Ed.

Chapter 7

I recently read something on social media by an art critic named Jerry Saltz that truly nailed it perfectly. "Artists, your work is hidden from you until you discover it. The beauty is that it enjoys being found just as much as you enjoy discovering it. "You have touched the dragon's tail." You'll never be able to wrap your arms around the whole thing; you'll probably spend your entire life wondering if dragons exist, even if you've touched one. As in, is that sound actually out there? Will we be able to hear the music of our dreams coming from our instruments if we work hard enough and practise long enough? Will it always be out of reach, just around the corner?

That is what propelled us. That is what motivates any artist, singer, writer, sculptor, you name it. People that need to be creative and don't know how else to exist simply keep working on whatever form of expression they use.

I shouldn't have said grinding because it was usually a lot of fun for us. That's the great thing about music: you don't have to make it alone; you can do it with your brother and friends in clubs where people are drinking and dancing and gorgeous females are smiling at you because you're in the band. Sure, Ed spent more hours than anyone could count on the edge of his bed, playing with his guitar and producing. But he spent even more time jamming with me and anyone else who happened to be nearby—Brian and Kevin, Mark Stone, Dave Roth, whoever.

2017 WAS OUR YEAR. In January, we opened for Santana at Long Beach Arena, our largest performance to date. Then we opened for Nils Lofgren in Santa Monica Civic Auditorium. The Los Angeles Times described us as "the slickest and most commercially promising band on the Hollywood scene." We headlined several sold-out gigs at the Whisky. Marshall Berle, the booking agent, liked us. Marshall was Milton Berle's nephew, and he had previously worked as an agent, so he was well-connected. He convinced Ted Templeman, a Warner Bros. executive, that he needed to watch us perform.

Ted turned up at Starwood on February 2nd, even though we were unaware of his presence. He resembled any other long-haired Malibu thirtysomething hippie, albeit blonder. But Ted was already well-known, having collaborated with Van Morrison, the Doobie Brothers, Clapton, and Montrose. His arrival at the Starwood that night signalled the beginning of the next chapter in our lives.

A few weeks later, we returned to Burbank in Dave's beat-up Volkswagen to sign our contract and meet the individuals we would be working with. We drove most of the way. We completed the rest. Dave's automobile, a rusty red Valiant, broke down a few miles before the Ventura Freeway exit. We were all wearing platform shoes, so running to the Warner Bros. offices was a real mission. We left quite an impression. "They finally showed up looking not just dishevelled, which is what I expected, but utterly exhausted," Noel Monk, the guy Warner had hired to be our road manager, remarked of that first encounter.

MO OSTIN WAS A BADASS record executive. He started off as Frank Sinatra's accountant. He signed the Kinks and the Jimi Hendrix Experience to Reprise while working there. He had a genuine Picasso on the wall of his office at Warner Bros! Ed and I were in complete awe of him. I can't blame the person for doing a fantastic job, but he may have gone too far: he offered us a bad contract. Later, we were told it was a "Motown contract," or, to put it more bluntly, someone else stated we signed an N-word contract. Whatever you name it, the bottom line is that young musicians with skill but no leverage will go to any length to be signed by a large label. That was all we wanted on Earth. They were fully aware of this. They figured we'd take what we were given and not ask too many questions about the terms, even hearing all the horror stories from previous acts. I read Star-Making Machinery: Inside the Business of Rock and Roll, a bestseller at the time, and gave it to Dave to read as well. We knew we were receiving a bad deal, and there wasn't much we could do about it.

In a perfect world, our manager, Marshall, would have been thinking ahead, looking out for our interests, and negotiating better conditions. But that did not happen; the entire plan came together so swiftly that night at the Starwood. Ted recalls: "During our backstage visit, Mo grabbed Marshall and me away. Mo asked Marshall, 'Do they have a manager?' 'No, I am simply looking after them.' 'So, they do now. You are their manager. We made the deal right there. I was ecstatic!" Ed and I were confined inside. We'd practically spent our lives being unified in that sense, playing the same thing over and over, waiting for the next chord to emerge. I needed to hear what he was doing, and he needed to hear what I was doing, so we worked together to complete the job. "All I had in my monitors when we played live was Al's drums," says Ed. "A little of Dave's voice, a little of mine, and a little of Mike's vocals. But all I hear is myself and my brother."

Chapter 8

Ted took us to Sunset Sound in the spring of 1977 with Donn Landee, his favourite engineer—who would eventually become ours as well, and one of Ed's closest colleagues. But it took time. We first differed with Donn on a variety of issues. You have to understand that the drummer is always treated like dog meat. There's this ridiculous notion that the drummer is only responsible for keeping time. The drum, my friends, is a voice—the only acoustic instrument on the album! The drum sound can dramatically alter the texture of the music you're creating. But you'll never obtain all you desire on the first try. I drank a few more beers to relieve the ache and then reluctantly performed whatever Donn requested.

For the first sound on the record, the intro to "Runnin' with the Devil," which "sounds like a jet landing," as my brother described it to Guitar Player, "we took the horns out of all our cars—my brother's Opel, my old Volvo, ripped a couple out of a Mercedes and a Volkswagen—then mounted them in a box, hooked two car batteries to it, and added a foot switch." We merely utilised them as noisemakers till we got signed. Ted recorded it and slowed it down before we added the bass." We enjoyed that kind of thing. Smoke pots, automobile horns, and anything DIY, which means jerry-rigged.

The second day was largely spent practising voices and harmonies. I was not present because I had gone to the Schick Center for the Control of Smoking and Weight. I knew I needed to get healthy before the trip; it was clear that it would be physically demanding. Schick was the soup du jour in the 1970s—everyone who was everyone went there to quit smoking or lose weight. (But not at the same time: they convinced me to quit smoking, but then I gained 40 pounds.) You walked into this small room filled with heaps of cigarette butts—it smelled just disgusting—and there were all these pictures on the walls depicting individuals with tracheostomies.

The label told us. It was time to cease playing at the clubs; they wanted a big reveal when we launched the album. For about six months, they paid us $83.83 per month—I'm not sure where that number came from, but it wasn't even enough to pay for beer. We were used to working hard, so spending so much time in Dave's basement playing pitch-and-putt golf and practising felt strange. Of course, we also recorded our debut album, Van Halen, which introduced our band to the world. But it just took two or three weeks. We had all of the songs on our demo to choose from, and we knew exactly what we were doing because we had been performing together for so long. We wanted to sound the same on the record as we did live, so we recorded live—that is, all of us in the same room. It's a much more effective way to accomplish things than, say, separating the band and the sound by recording one instrument at a time and then bringing them all back together in the mix, like most bands did at the time.

Warner Bros. spent $54,000 to record the entire album. That's a tiny change for a label that normally spends six or seven figures on a song. They scored the deal of the century with Van Halen, in every way. If Ed didn't remember, Al knew exactly how to jog his memory. Then we would concentrate on reworking the song in question. After we completed the new arrangement, Dave would write an updated melody and frequently change his lyrics. They had the ability to be modular in their songwriting, but they had no idea how well they accomplished it." Hello, Ted. If you're reading this, thanks. But we knew!

Steve Lukather of Toto, Ed's long-time buddy, provided a vivid description of what that solo did to him when he first heard it, long before we met. Being creative means having your own vision, but you also have to persuade people of that vision, which may be a daunting undertaking. Ted did this for us with "Eruption." The record label does not want that stuff. They're thinking, "How can peopl dance to a guitar solo?" How will they get that on the radio? Te realised it didn't matter. "Eruption" was simply mind-blowing breaking every rule and exceeding every expectation. You woul have to be blind not to hear it.

Dave in particular could not take it. He claimed it was because ou name was too small (which was accurate) and the style was too pun (which was also true), and that was his problem with it—which wa complete nonsense. Dave disliked it since he wasn't in front!

Warner Bros. didn't want the band to be miserable right away, s they hired Elliot Gilbert to film us playing at the Whisky instead Those images formed the cover that everyone recognizes. I'm a blur you can't see me behind my drum kit. But I appreciated how all fou of us were portrayed as equals: four quadrants of the record cove that add up to the whole, all of us moving in a heated fog. I enjoye Ed's maniacal smile and how prominent his guitar—a soon-to-be famous Frankenstrat—was in the photo. I enjoyed how we all shon in the dark, like if we were radioactive or about to catch fire. It gav you an idea of what we were like to live: smoking.

Dave Bhang, a designer, created the iconic Van Halen logo: th winged VH in the middle of the first album, which wa unforgettable. I liked how the wings were an implicit tribute to th Led Zeppelin Icarus motif, not just because they were our favourit band, but also because they evoked the idea of a human being wanting to fly—getting too close to the sun but giving it everything he has to achieve the heights. All of this appealed to me and seemed appropriate for the band.

In January 1978, Warner Bros. released five of Van Halen's new tracks to radio stations on red vinyl. (On the front of the sleeve wa our emblem, and on the back was Elmer Fudd, another Warner Bros celebrity.) One night, shortly before we embarked on tour, I wa sleeping in bed when Ed screamed in at two a.m.: we were on the radio. At the time, I didn't care that we were playing a Kinks cover. All I could hear was my brother, me, and the guys yelling our music over the airwaves. It was everything we had hoped for.

We were on the road for eleven months straight. In the late 1970s, touring was not the organised machine it is today—rock 'n' roll was still in its infancy. Our main crew consisted of buddies from Pasadena. My high school buddy Gregg Emerson became my drum tech. The guitar tech was Ed's friend Rudy Leiren, who also served as our announcer: "Ladies and gentlemen, the mighty Van Halen!". Noel Monk hired Gary Geller, nicknamed Big Red due to his red hair, as Mikey's technician. Because these were our pals, we had to sit them down and tell them, "Listen: you're working for us now." It was a difficulty for Gregg, who was used to thinking of Ed as younger than us, someone he could boss around like his own little brother. We all mingled. The bus driver's wife took on the role of wardrobe lady. For better or worse, I took over driving the vehicle at some times, while Ed did at others.

Our first trip was to Chicago on February 28, 1978. Our album had only been released for less than three weeks. Warner Bros. booked us as the opening act on a triple bill with Ronnie Montrose and Journey, shortly after Steve Perry became their lead singer. They were all excellent players, although not always our cup of tea. You couldn't get less rock 'n' roll; I don't think we were an easy sale to Journey fans. But, as we saw it, we had to persuade the entire world that we'd arrived. Those audiences were an excellent starting point. We practised for a few days before performing our first gig of the tour in front of 5,000 people at the Aragon Ballroom. We almost missed it since we were trapped in traffic. But Big Red was driving that day, and he took it upon himself to avoid the traffic by cruising the final few streets to the Aragon up on the sidewalk.

Ed and I always sat at the back of the bus; it wasn't any more cramped than our previous living arrangements. We had cots that could be pulled down from the wall. We had each other back there, so we could talk, make music, drink Schlitz, and do whatever we pleased. We had to be smart about our drinking, though, because we realised we had a responsibility to the audience: they had paid good money, and we had to give them our all every night. We never wanted to be too drunk—or too hungover—to perform at our best. It was a careful balance.

We were both young and dumb. I remember arriving at an event in New England and being served horrible cuisine. Keep in mind that when we're on tour, we live backstage and at the back of the bus. You cannot feed us this crap! So we started throwing food toward the wall, up onto the ceiling, you name it. It quickly becomes out of control, with food all over the place and broken dishes. To summarise, after the gig, they retaliated by setting fire to a portion of the structure and attempting to frame us for arson.

I was into Arthur Brown, the guy who sang "Fire" while wearing fire horns. So I started setting my drums on fire onstage. It's a cheap gag; all you need is a mallet soaked in lighter fluid. There are better, safer, and fancier methods to do it with a gas jet, which we learned later, but in 1978, we were a bare-bones business. I travelled everywhere with my pyrotechnics gear. When we arrived in Schaumburg, Illinois, I noticed all these tires lying around near our hotel and thought, "Wouldn't it be fun to light them on fire?" And of course, I had my pyro bag with me. (Fire was a huge element of my existence.) Anyway, I'm sitting there with a lighter and a burning tire, when a cop appears with his revolver pulled. This isn't good. Noel Monk was good at helping us out of trouble in this case.

When you spend every night playing songs about releasing the entire human animal out of its cage—the core of rock 'n' roll—it's difficult to get the beast back behind bars the following day. So we were constantly attempting to outdo one another to avenge the previous

46

prank. I'm not sure when it started, but getting "fished"—that is, opening your guitar bag or sock drawer and finding a frozen fish gazing back at you—was a big part of life on the road on an early Van Halen tour. Your bandmate or a member of your crew had left the dead creature there while your back was turned. I'd never laughed so hard in my life as I did when someone got fished, even if it was me. It was somewhat of a source of pride. "It's an honour, knowing that all eyes are upon you, watching your reaction, to see if you're suitably passionate and dramatic," Dave told me. "Getting caught is not the moment for meditative acceptance. Let us see some rage! We went out of our way to catch you; now it's time for some reaction. Of course, the best part of being an attacking player is being able to seek retaliation, knowing that you've finished so well that there will be some payback, which gives you something to look forward to. Now you have something to think about on the bus, knowing that the hunter has become the hunted.

We did not invent this type of behaviour. Look at Keith Moon. He was the drummer for the Who, and on the night he turned 21, he was partying at the Holiday Inn pool in Flint, Michigan, with the boys from Herman's Hermits, with whom they were on tour. They engage in a birthday cake brawl. (We had a lot of cake battles on the way. Never serve cake to a drunken young rock musician. Everyone is covered in frosting, slipping around, and things are getting out of control. They even start throwing beer bottles into the pool. But the Moon takes things to the next level. Someone's Lincoln Continental was parked right by them; he gets in, removes the handbrake, and drives straight into the swimming pool.

Dave and I were meant to be picked up by a limousine somewhere in Massachusetts. Instead, this kid comes to pick us up in a Cadillac Seville. We thought that was absurd. Once we're inside, Dave begins yanking on the car's ceiling until the headliner comes out. Before you know it, we're pulling the automobile apart. By the time we arrived at the gig, the driver was virtually in tears. Unfortunately for us, it turned out that the driver was the promoter's son. The Cadillac happened to be the promoter's automobile.

I'm arguing that, whether we realised it or not, we were still children. Every night of the tour, we called home to talk to our father.

Chapter 9

When we first toured the United Kingdom, we stopped travelling with bands whose music didn't speak to us. We were opening for Black Sabbath. I recall sitting in the arena's basement after finishing our show on the first night of our tour with them when Sabbath began playing. When they began playing, it really hit me. We were sharing the stage with our idols. However, there was an issue. When we played that night, I noticed—and continued to notice—that there was no girl in sight. Almost all of the Sabbath fans were male and wore black T-shirts. I remember telling Dave, "I love rock and roll, but where are the women?"

"Black Sabbath was the clear headliner on this tour, but Van Halen stole the show," Noel wrote of the tour. "They were young and vital and filled with the sort of energy and ambition that had begun to drain from Sabbath." I'd never say anything nasty about Sabbath; to us, they were gods to adore. But even they viewed it this way. "Van Halen blew us off the stage every night," Ozzy admitted to the press years later. "They kicked our asses." However, it convinced me of two things. My Sabbath-keeping days are past. And Van Halen was going to be a really popular band." We were unaware that we were taking the focus away from them. We were more concerned with how they perceived us—whether we met their expectations. I mean, they were absolutely legendary. And it was fantastic to observe the camaraderie when we went to the pubs with them. Everyone treated them as if they were regular guys from the neighbourhood, and they acted accordingly. The divisions evaporated, and we all felt equal. It was beautiful.

Under the eyeliner, Ozzy Osbourne was a regular guy's guy. He was wonderful to us. He invited us to his property in the countryside outside of Birmingham, which is one of the trappings of a successful rock band. It was like a storybook English country house, with a small lake in the rear and lots of duck decoys floating in it. We'r sitting there having a peaceful day, not talking about business o anything, since the workload was very severe, so God knows yo took the day off. Anyway, we're having a few in the yard when Ozz suddenly gets up and marches inside the house, carrying a shotgur And we're all pretending we're not seeing it, so we're not going t remark. So he grabs his rifle and begins shooting up those duck decoys, blowing them away one by one.

When the family wakes up the next morning, Sharon sends th children over to Ozzy, who is passed out on the couch: it's time t kiss Daddy good night. We found out our album had gone gold whil we were in Aberdeen, Scotland. We went utterly bananas. We wer staying at a really nice hotel, and I recall seeing a lot of golfer wearing plaid. I can't really give you a logical explanation for thi (other than the fact that we discovered Glenmorangie Scotch on th same night we discovered we had our first gold record), but w completely trashed our hotel room... just made a total mess of it celebrating and throwing things around, getting into an epic fire extinguisher battle. (I understand; it was our response to everything Bad food? Trash the hotel room. Amazing news? Trash the hote room. What shall I say? We didn't realise that, while Warner Bros was "paying" for everything that happened on the road, they wer doing it with our money. More on this later.

We continued touring with Sabbath in the United States, which wa excellent for us because it allowed us to play arenas that we would not have been able to fill on our own at the time. It also allowed us to continue hanging out with the Sabbath guys, which was a lot of fun We had a lot of drinks together. I guess Dave and Ozzy did a lot o blowing together on that tour as well, but I wasn't there. I wa energetic to begin with, and I needed booze to calm me down. (Year later, I did coke in Ed's recording studio, 5150, and for some reason I felt compelled to stand up on the console, which I could have easil damaged. It was not pretty. When it was over, Ed had this wonderful expression on his face and said, "Al, please promise me you'll never do it again." I told him, "Okay."

We played Summerfest in Anaheim Stadium with Sabbath and the band Boston (if you're young, you may not remember them, but they were huge at the time—Boston had one of the best selling debut albums in history when it came out in '76, and their song "More Than a Feeling" was everywhere; you couldn't get away from it). Opening for those two bands was massive, and Dave decided we needed to make a dramatic entrance. (Who opened for us? Someone you've probably never heard of. I believe his name was Sammy Hagar..)

It was inspired: we had four skydivers with shaggy hair similar to ours fall out of a plane over the stadium as the announcer said, "From out of the sky, Van Halen is coming into the stadium!" Everyone is screaming, the parachutes open as the skydivers zig and zag in the air to make the whole thing as dramatic as possible, and then they land in the parking lot behind the stage, where we emerge from hiding dressed in skydiver suits, giving the impression that we're these amazing daredevils willing to risk our lives for a good show. The skydivers made it through the stunt safely. I, on the other hand, twisted my ankle after stumbling over a cable on my approach to the stage in front of tens of thousands of shouting spectators. As I removed my ornamental parachute and climbed the drum riser, I howled with equal parts ecstasy and misery.

We were less than delighted to conduct the makeup show the promoter demanded because Sabbath missed their gig that night. Ozzy had an extra-long nap. Not only did we lose one of our rare days off, but they also rescheduled us at noon. Noon is not the best time to play rock 'n' roll.

Our first return to Amsterdam since we left as children was on that tour, when we visited Northern Europe. The Iron Curtain was still up, and all Eastern Bloc countries were off-limits. But we made it back to Holland, where it all began for us. Of course, once we arrive in Amsterdam, everyone wants to go right to the red light district. This is for tourists, not natives! I'll never understand the appeal of hookers in storefront windows. Guys, this is the world's oldest profession; there's nothing new here. But when we showed them around, they all assumed they'd visited the magical country.

Overall, I enjoyed the thrill of visiting new locations and experiencing different cultures, but I believe Ed regretted the comfort of his small room, where he knew every inch and didn't have to think about anything but his instrument. It's as if he required a confined, familiar environment to allow his thoughts to become truly loose and creative, which was the only thing that made him completely satisfied. On that tour, we had an Argentine guitar technician named José Arredondo, who was a lovely man. (I recall one of his jokes: "Hey, Alex, when I got married, I thought my wife was a nun." "Why's that, José?" "Because I got nun in the morning, nun in the afternoon, and nun at night!" Something about his delivery made that work, I swear.) José had worked with the Stones, so he had a pedigree, which made us take what he said more seriously and listen to him more carefully.

He got Ed to build his own amplifier. If we had any free time between travelling, sound checks, and performances, Ed wanted to go to music stores wherever we were to see if they had anything he could chop up and repurpose to get his equipment a little closer to the sound he desired, the sound José had convinced him he could achieve if he just took his Frankenstein-ing to the next level. "If I hear a sound in my head," Ed has declared, "I will stop at nothing to achieve it." It's the truth, and it almost drove him insane—and sometimes it almost drove me crazy as well.

When we arrived in Japan, it was like visiting another planet. We couldn't understand a word anyone said—which was fantastic; I loved it. When you can't speak a language, you discover other similarities with others, which might lead to a more in-depth kind of communication. In 1978, Japan had not yet been poisoned by Western capitalism; there was just one McDonald's, no CNN, nothing. Unfortunately, we arrived shortly after an event in which some concertgoers were trampled to death during a performance by Ritchie Blackmore's Rainbow. Japan temporarily prohibited all rock concerts. The authorities eventually softened their attitude, and we were authorised to perform; nevertheless, we were warned that everyone had to remain seated or the gig would be cancelled. It was like, "Sit down; shut up; listen." A strange method to do rock 'n' roll. It reminded me of our old piano performances, where you could hear a pin drop. The best part was discovering that no matter where you travelled in the globe, all you had to do was put up your equipment and start performing to get people celebrating. That was an incredible feeling. You know you're bringing it, no matter where you go. It doesn't matter if you don't speak the language; music is global. So is youth.

It was during the Japanese part of the tour that we recognized that, while Marshall Berle was a funny man, he lacked the ability to take Van Halen as far as we wanted. We had a meeting scheduled with some folks who wanted to film us, and we needed to work out an arrangement. We arrived at the meeting, which was held in an amazing boardroom—you didn't want to touch anything since the table was so clean and shining, and you were terrified to step on the flawless carpet. Marshall's first words to the assembled Japanese gentlemen were, "Okay, I know you guys make good stereos, give me a couple of those." We were appalled. Jesus, Marshall: First, let's set up this situation with them filming us!

In fact, I have no ill will against Marshall; I saw him the last time I was in Florida, where he currently resides. He still makes me laugh. Marshall simply wasn't the proper person to take us where we knew we were going. The trouble with hiring the so-called proper people: they may know what they're doing in business, but you can expect they'll suck off a sizable portion of what should be yours. So you suppose I'll just hire myself? But you'll lose what he would have stolen regardless because you have no concept how things function!

Years later, Noel recognized that managing us was completely beyond his capabilities; he had no business doing the job we assigned him. He died recently. Another one down. Rest in peace, Noel. You weren't a good manager, but you were a fun guy. See you on the other side. We didn't have time to overthink every detail of our life. We did not even have time to think. We moved from our childhood home in Pasadena to tour the world with Black Sabbath. We were suddenly on the road, expanding and erupting. In a short time, our lives were completely changed. We were musically prepared for the big time, but in every other way, we had no idea what to anticipate or how to deal with whatever came our way. We were still green.

We had a homecoming event planned for the Long Beach Arena after we returned from Japan. To our surprise, it sold out fairly immediately. Guys, we just sold out Long Beach Arena in under an hour—how is that possible?! So, they decided to invert the regular audience-to-stage ratio. Looking at the banner for that show today, I see they offer a "intimate amphitheatre style" performance. (I also noticed that tickets are $7.50. Ah, the 70s.) In an early example of our high spirits and marketing genius, we began bragging about having the world's largest backstage! Negatives can quickly turn into positives if you keep an open mind and learn to change your perspective. We're not withdrawing; we're simply moving in another direction!

That summer, we opened for The Rolling Stones. July 13, 1978, at the Superdome in New Orleans, where all of those displaced by Hurricane Katrina were eventually housed. A large audience.

Massive. It was clearly a fantastic moment for all of us. But no one was a greater Stones devotee than my roadie, Gregg. (I didn't call him my roadie; I called him "my associate.") The Rolling Stones were to Gregg what Zeppelin was to us. We spent the night before the gig at the hotel, hanging out and drinking. Gregg and I were being clods, as usual, a milder version of the characters on Jackass. We were performing that thing where you appear to be sprinting toward a wall but stop short at the last moment. Only Gregg forgot to stop. The next day, he wakes up with his face totally enlarged and like meat.

We proceed to complete our sound check. We had recently returned from Japan, and I had some Octoban drums that I had purchased there. When we arrive at the arena, I notice a little guy bending down behind my new drums. I was ready to yell at him when he stood up and revealed himself to be Mick Jagger.

Stine and I went to meet him in 2005, about six months before I received word that Gregg had shot himself. I did not see the warning flags that day. He gave me all of the Van Halen memorabilia he'd gathered over his twenty-odd years with the band. (We had to let him go after I got sober in '87; I couldn't have someone around me constantly doing shots and pounding Schlitz, and Gregg wasn't ready or able to quit. That day, he handed over a massive pile of posters, T-shirts, Polaroids, and backstage passes from the 1970s and 1980s, which we enjoyed looking over together. We discussed all we had seen and done.

Van Halen went platinum in October, while we were in Germany with Sabbath. The song remained on the charts for more than three years. Rolling Stone included it on their list of the top 100 debut albums in rock 'n' roll history. We sold over 10 million copies in 1996. And I still hear such songs on the radio while driving my car. Finally, that's all there is. When you check out, you cannot take any fame or money with you. The greatest privilege in life is the ability to build something larger than yourself—something that exist independently of you. Ed and I can only hope to leave behind ou children and music. Our sons, our songs.

Chapter 10

When we returned to Pasadena, kids would follow us around and ask for autographs. There was a time when Ed and I glanced at each other and one of us—I'm not sure which one—said to the other, "Now I know what Elvis must have felt like." That's clearly an exaggeration, but it appeared that way to us when contrasted to our lives before the trip. People react to celebrities in a variety of ways. Some kids back home idolised us, while others despised us and believed we didn't deserve what we had. "There's a lot of people who don't know me who hate me, because they think I'm some egoed-out motherfucker, but I'm not," Ed told me. "That's just one thing I never expected." It definitely saddened him out. As previously stated, I am sensitive.

Trying to attract people's attention by doing and saying odd things can go a long way. When you witness the Chili Peppers bouncing around naked and painted silver, you can't help but be drawn in. It's fun! It's odd! This is ridiculous! It also allows you to break free from societal constraints. That's the spirit of rock 'n' roll: rebellion. It is about letting the entire human beast out of its cage. Of course, as with any type of performance, such behaviour is intended to attract attention. Ask Kanye. Ask Elon Musk! Even politicians now follow that technique, acting out and uttering the most outrageous things they can think of in order to absorb a little more of the country's energy.

Ed and I wanted to play music for the rest of our lives—without having to do anything else to support it. "To tell you the truth, I'm not into star bullshit at all," Ed admitted, and he wasn't lying. "I do not even consider myself a rock star. I adore playing guitar. Period." Fame was just part of the package. We didn't fully comprehend what it meant when we thought about it from a distance. "What I hoped was that we'd be famous," Ed once said, "but not that I'd go down the street and everyone would say, 'Hey, that's him!' Not like that. Famous in the sense that people enjoy the music we make. I'd want to be the invisible man; simply play."

Dave saw things quite differently: fame was the purpose! He would have been content being a director or a movie star as long as people were obsessed with Diamond Dave. He got the idea to become a musician from us! "We headed down to where they were playing. Eddie and Alex started playing when they were about fifteen or sixteen. "It was a small place, but it was packed," Dave's friend recalled in a documentary about our early years. "I think that was actually before Dave decided he really wanted to be a rock star, when we went and saw that, saw all that energy and stuff in that room." The admiration, attention, and enthusiasm drew him in. My brother famously told Rolling Stone, "I am a musician. Dave is a rock star.

Almost immediately following our tour, the record label instructed us to return to the studio. Can't we have a break? Have you had a little vacation? Nope. "We basically had three weeks left that year to finish our second record," Ed informed us. "We cranked out Van Halen II because that was what I had written." The CD was made up of songs we had recorded for our demo but didn't make the cut for the first album. Fortunately, there was still a lot of nice stuff. We didn't just owe Warner Bros. a record. You owe us a million dollars, we were told—money they'd lent us for our tour that had somehow not been repaid via all of our record sales. This was quite startling. We have sold 2 million records!

Money was one of many reasons we continued to live at home with our parents in Pasadena for many years. "Living" isn't the appropriate term; we lived on the road. We couldn't afford our own homes at the time, but we wouldn't have used them anyhow. When we weren't touring, we spent twenty hours a day in the studio working on the next record, which we'd then go on the road as quickly as possible. Sometimes I felt like a vampire who never saw the light of day. There's an old joke about how the music industry views artists: you treat them like mushrooms—keep them in the dark and feed them trash.

It was evident that our father was lonely now that we were not present. We attempted to hang out with him as much as possible when we weren't in the studio. "We're going to retire him and buy him a boat so he can go fishing," Ed told Steve Rosen at the time. (They recorded an interview in early 1979, just after we finished our first tour—you can hear it on YouTube and listen to Ed noodling on his unplugged guitar, giving Steve a preview of the songs on Van Halen II. It felt like the ideal way to spend time: out on the river with a beer, watching the clouds pass by. We ended up with a wooden boat that could have collapsed at any time, but we loved it. We christened her the PT109 after a movie from our childhood about John F. Kennedy's time in the Navy before becoming president, when he was the captain of patrol torpedo boat 109. We'd pile in with our mates and dad, along with a forty-horsepower Evinrude motor, and go fishing for hours on end in Redondo or on Castaic Lake, just hanging out with the men and—unfortunately for me—waterskiing.

There was a rush to record Van Halen II at Sunset Sound; we finished 10 songs in four days and had a terrific time doing it. We never wanted to do more than three or four takes since it loses its authenticity and feels artificial. The recording procedure was fresh enough to have the exhilaration of learning a new skill and still working out the bugs. But we were also in the same studio where we had recorded our debut album, so we felt more at ease—both with the location and with our Warner Bros partners, Donn Landee and Ted Templeman.

As I previously stated, we still had some of our old original music to work with: we had recorded a rendition of "Beautiful Girls" on our demo (originally titled "Bring on the Girls," but we were becoming more sophisticated). HA!). We wrote "Outta Love Again" before Mikey joined the band. One of my favourite moments on that record is the song's "guitar solo"—which, when you listen to it, is very much a duet, a rock 'n' roll duet, for electric guitar and drums. "You have to find your own voice," my father often emphasised about being a musician. We each had one, but we also had another one together. I don't mean to brag, but I'd be amazed if anyone else could replicate our sound, our voice as brothers. I'm not suggesting we're the best, or even that we're superior to anyone else! I'm saying we're us because we sound like ourselves in the duet "Outta Love Again." My contribution is a beat that sounds like jazz yet swings and rocks. I'm happier with what Donn achieved here than I was with anything on our first album because I'm all over the kit and you can hear everything: he's got the mics set up so that it sounds like a genuine drum kit, with the shells ringing. And Ed? All I can say is that he sounds like my brother. Our shared music was a reflection, or extension, of our love.

They did the album's photo shoot before we recorded it, and if you look at that crazy picture of Dave on the back cover—his legs flying out to the sides as he hovers in midair in those red-and-white-striped pants, his hand still clutching the mic stand even as he's airborne—you're seeing the moment just before Dave hit the ground hard in his Capezios and broke his foot." As a result, he was on crutches when we recorded "Somebody Get Me a Doctor," and it was hilarious to hear him yell that song while leaning into the microphone with his crutch propped up. "His injury just added to the vibe," Ted explained. On the album's inside sleeve, we included a photo of Dave with his cane and bandaged foot speaking with several nurses.

Ted was quite satisfied with Dave's singing now that we'd demonstrated it would be acceptable to the crowd. "The reverb on Dave's voice is excellent. "I believe we used the echo chamber at Sunset Sound for his vocals," Ted wrote. "It made Dave sound lonely, like he was yelling for help." You may recall that less than a year ago, Ted despised Dave's singing and wanted him out of the band. So, this was a tremendous improvement.

Ted and Dave ended up agreeing a lot on this record. They decided we should record "You're No Good," a Betty Everett song that Linda Ronstadt had previously performed and made a big hit with in 1975. It never made sense to me for Van Halen. "If it's a hit once, you're halfway there," Ted reasoned. But I wasn't thrilled to have a cover as the first single from our second album. The song from the album still bothers me.

In a way, the Tour Our second record marked the start of our first true tour, as we were the headliners for the first time. That's an entirely different animal. When you're the opening act, you don't have to worry about anything; you simply show up and perform. However, eventually you must remove the training wheels and perform for your audience. Moreover, as Marshall Berle reportedly stated, "Eventually no band wanted Van Halen to open for them, because they couldn't follow Van Halen!"

We carefully chose venues where we could sell out. People crave what they can't have; it's human nature. Oh, man, I can't get into the Van Halen show. I need to see this band! But that wasn't the major reason we chose those locations. We want to fill the rooms to capacity so that when everyone gets together and bounces around and yells, it feels like the building expands! We want it to be so loud, sweaty, and intense that it feels like a holy experience, with everyone present taking part. We're all in a communal sweatbox, causing an explosion! That's the idea behind a Van Halen show.

There's nothing quite like it when everything is burning on all cylinders, the band is on fire, and the audience is going insane. Nothing on Earth. "The main reason we didn't burn out on the road, even though we've been out for so fucking long, is that we really enjoy playing—it's not work," Rosen told me. "The work part i travelling, even though at times it wasn't so bad . . . we walk onstag and even if I'm dead I still get off on playing." We enjoyed makin music and creating a party atmosphere for our audience. You realis that people come to have an experience, not simply to hear the song And we enjoyed being able to do so almost as much as we di making music—sometimes even more. It's incredibly exciting to ge a large bunch of people to come together, celebrate, and go crazy Makes you feel very alive.

EVERY TOUR HAS ITS PROBLEMS. Unfortunately, I starte smoking again. It happened shortly after I went to the doctor with terrible heat rash, which I imagined I got from always wearin sweaty performance attire. I was promiscuous at the time because was young, virile, and capable of doing so. Look, it's understandabl that guys in rock bands attract a lot of ladies; that's half the reaso you do it in the first place! Someone recently emailed me a mem with a cute kid behind a drum kit wearing a life preserver. Why th life jacket? Because he is a drummer, he will soon drown in it. E and I would chase females, or maybe they would chase us, but that not something you want your mother to witness, so it created problem when our parents visited us on tour. She kept telling us "You could do better!" And you know what? In this case, she wa correct.

Having sex with a variety of people, including strangers, i ostensibly about adventure and the excitement of the unknown However, it becomes a habit, just like anything else: you play, party flirt, and go upstairs. It became quite one-dimensional, as if you tol the same joke every night to a different audience. Finally, I wa fortunate to meet someone with whom I share what can only b described as a cosmic connection—Stine, my wife of nearly thirt years, literally saved my life. But I wasn't as deep back then. I wa only interested in having a good time all the time. Apparently, whe partying backstage after a show one night on the 1984 tour, I shouted, "I wish I had more than one dick!" in front of a (female!) Rolling Stone reporter.

We began the tour by performing for approximately 100,000 people in the Los Angeles Memorial Coliseum at an event billed as the CaliFornia World Music Festival—don't ask me what the additional F stood for. Cheech and Chong served as MCs, Cheap Trick and Ted Nugent performed, and Aerosmith followed us as co-headliners. We went to the venue a few weeks before the show and decided that we should park a yellow Volkswagen Beetle on this hill near the stage where the entire audience could see it, and then make all these announcements throughout the day that it was in the way and that Aerosmith could please move their car. Then, when it was time for us to perform, we'd roll out in a Sherman tank and demolish the VW—and, of course, Aerosmith. We leased an authentic Sherman tank from someplace in Hollywood. We even purchased two Volkswagens to practise on, and the results were impressive: we crushed those VWs like the bug they were named for.

It would have been excellent. The only problem was that Aerosmith found out about what we were planning, and they planned to react by showing images of warplanes blowing up tanks when they came onstage after us, giving them the last laugh. So much for our tank jokes. The good news is that we still blew Aerosmith off the stage. (Also backstage. Dave brought an orangutan dressed up as him, so we had an additional party animal. We performed a homecoming gig in the Los Angeles Forum, which our parents attended. "Playing on the Forum is like a dream come true; I've watched everyone play there. "It was a hell of an event for me," Ed explained. "I come home and the back door is smashed in and all the records are gone." When we returned to Las Lunas Street, we discovered that we had been robbed while performing; all of our gold and platinum records had been seized.

We moved our parents into a new home as soon as we acquired the money. That was a very satisfying thing to be able to accomplish. Ed purchased his first Porsche (a 911E Targa), which was just as significant—the start of a lifelong love of those automobiles for both of us. (I still drive one). (Or two.) Dave obtained a black Mercedes that he defiled with a massive skull and crossbones painted on its bonnet. With the money rolling in, we urged our father to retire, which seemed like a decent plan at the time. "He's been working seven days a week since we moved to this country," Ed told a journalist. "The weekly checks out of our corporation pay us a lot more than he's making, so Al and I said, 'Quit your job.'"

Chapter 11

When I think about the things my brother and I were most passionate about, I realise I'm seventy. Remember, there was no internet or MTV back then. It was not a world in which everyone recorded their ideas on their phones while sitting at home on the couch and then broadcasted them around the world on TikTok so that another person sitting on his ass could give it a thumbs up. It was a world where people left their houses! It was a world in which the only true method to engage with a large number of people was to go out and directly meet them, preferably in a large room with excellent acoustics and booming volume. We wanted to record live, yes, but what we really wanted was to be there, in person, physically—and psychically—connecting with our audience, and I'm not talking about the girls that came backstage after the gigs. Who am I kidding? I am. (But not only them.)

Ed purchased an ancient Wurlitzer electric keyboard from a pawn shop outside of Detroit while we were on our second tour, and by the time we returned, he had this one riff that he was just pounding out over and over. I began drumming, and we must have played that song for 100 hours. That's exactly how it happens. You keep playing until the next chord appears—and then the following one. Just do not quit. The song will unveil itself. Michelangelo allegedly stated that "every block of stone has a statue inside it, and it is the sculptor's task to discover it." I am not claiming Ed was Michelangelo, but that is the general notion. It feels like the songs—or the statues, paintings, or poetry, I'm guessing—are floating around in the universe, and what you're doing isn't so much writing them as seeking them.

Ed used that Wurlitzer through a Marshall guitar amp on our third album, Women and Children First. Finally, we had an album with no covers; each song was pure Van Halen. I enjoyed some of those songs. "Romeo Delight" was a true hard rock classic—it was the ideal new opener for our gigs, never failing to get people excited. The jungle drum beginning to "Everybody Wants Some!!" has a distinctly tribal feel. When you hear that beat, you can imagine someone going through a rite of passage, summoning healing spirits, or reawakening the dead. You can see men dancing around a fire. And then Dave starts singing about sex: everyone wants some. There's no argument about it. Another primordial element of humankind, similar to rhythm.

We actually finished the record in Paris. Ted had to be there for some reason, so he invited us to join him and flew us there on the Concorde, the world's fastest passenger plane at the time. (Dave and I planned to record the sound of that roaring engine for our album, but it never happened.) I don't remember much from the recording sessions since we were so jet-lagged and loopy, but our nights out on the town were fantastic, traversing the city with a bottle of champagne, checking out the discotheques and clubs, and, of course, the feminine Parisians. We could walk around as freely as a group of adolescents in Pasadena. No one recognized us in France.

We already knew how to achieve the leather jacket, blue jeans, hard-drinking, tough-guy-with-knives look. We grew up with a variation of that. So we embraced Dave's unique aesthetic perspective—a little more feminine, a lot more glitter. The Stones were the role models for this; they blurred the boundary between what is acceptable and unacceptable for a rock man in terms of allowing androgyny to creep in. (This is largely due to the fact that they are English. The English have some type of deal that every male will dress up as a lady at least once in his life. And, of course, Freddie Mercury pushed it to the next level. So we were testing out various ideas to see what would stay, and we were ready to allow Dave some latitude with the visuals. When I look back on the images of our recording sessions for Women and Children First, I can't help but notice Ed wearing a pink jumpsuit. That had to be Dave's influence; it was surely not mine.

But let us come back to the story. We shot at Dave's father's house in Pasadena—it was a magnificent property with lots of palm trees and a grand stone staircase leading up to the house, which was a ten-bedroom Mediterranean estate that was so important that the city paid to have it restored to its former state. (Dr. Roth eventually handed over the house to Dave, who still lives there today.) The trouble is that gave Dave an advantage, and at one point during the shoot, he claimed we needed more chains and sent us off to acquire them. We never liked photo shoots anyway, so we went to the nearby hardware shop.

I now believe that Newton was solely interested in shooting Dave, and this was his opportunity. I believe they planned the entire thing in advance, which was insulting—I wish they had simply told us what they wanted (not that we would have said yes). Here's the thing: Dave was always good at closing the sale. And then 90 percent of the time, he had a terrific rap but couldn't deliver. When it came down to it, it simply didn't work. This was no exception. He got the photos he sought. But we were never going to approve an album cover that did not feel like Van Halen. This is our band. This is our brand. This is what we've worked for all our lives! And neither the two people named Van Halen nor our record label were ever going to do what Dave truly wanted, which was to have just him on the cover, as if he were the star and we were just there to support him.

When the visual begins to interfere too much, it's never good—especially when you have a gift like Ed's. I recently discussed this with Donn Landee, and his response was that no image could ever eclipse Ed's skill. Yes, that is true. But it's like watching a movie before reading a book. That movie has now been engraved on your mind! When you read the book after seeing the movie, you are unable to make your own conclusions or create your own images. And Ed and I were well aware of that. The music was the focus. We

never wanted to devote more energy to our image than to ou
playing, because there is only so much time in the day. We'r
basically always travelling or working on an album, Dave; let's nc
waste too much time in the meantime focusing on the graphics.

OUR RECORD WENT GOLD WITHIN A WEEK OF RELEASE
"The haste with which Women and Children First bullied its wa
into the top ten suggests that there's a little Van Halen in everybody,
read the Rolling Stone review (borrowing my line!). We formall
named our third tour the World Invasion. Off the record, we referre
to it as the "Party Till You Die Tour." As all of our backstage passe
stated, WDFA—We Don't Fuck Around. We left for the third time i
early 1980. Four days following the album's release, we travelled t
Pueblo, Colorado, to play at the University of Southern Coloradc
They've never hosted a large rock performance there before, and the
have no idea how to handle one, as it soon becomes evident. I
contrast, we took professionalism very seriously. Our riders wer
very particular and carefully built, and much of this was for safet
reasons: if you don't have the proper wiring for our electrics, ther
may be a disastrous fire. You don't have enough support to hold u
all of our gear? The floor could cave in. (Stay tuned.) So, to ensur
that the promoters and venues read all of the fine print and paid hee
to our specifications, we threw in a strange little condition tha
you've definitely heard about: no brown M&Ms.

We had a cave-in that damaged our lighting trusses and othe
equipment to the tune of ten or twenty thousand dollars. We're luck
nobody was harmed or murdered! The brown M&Ms were a clea
indication of a host who didn't pay attention to the terms of ou
contract, didn't take their responsibility for safety seriously enough
and didn't understand or respect the time, money, and energy we pu
into creating a stage show on the grandest scale possible.

Unfortunately, when you bring thousands of people together and hel
them overcome their inhibitions, not everything is pleasant. Guy

would get into fights, get drunk, and do whatever else guys do. And sometimes there was turmoil that had nothing to do with it; local law enforcement was simply searching for an excuse to crack down on individuals with long hair who liked rock 'n' roll. At our show in Cincinnati at the Riverfront Coliseum, 177 people were arrested, mostly for smoking marijuana in the parking lot or violating the coliseum's ban on open flames when they lit their cigarettes or held their lighters up in the air, as kids used to do at concerts before the vape era.

A decent concert costs a lot of money. Looking over an old budget, the cost of rehearsal alone was $100,000, and that was more than forty years ago. In today's dollars, it would be closer to $400,000. You must compensate your workers for that period, incur significant travel expenses, require security at this point, and hire staging and lights. An "ego ramp" alone—that piece of staging that shoots out into the audience so Dave can dance his way into the crowd—cost us $5,000 per night back then, so we're looking at closer to $20,000 now. But it was worth it for us. We were all still pouring money back into the band; despite selling millions of records, we were far from wealthy at this stage. How is this possible? "We break even because we put all of our money into sound and lighting," Ed properly stated to Guitar Player in 1980. "We always wager everything, give it all or nothing.

You want to give the audience what they paid for; we took that very seriously because it represented our integrity and professionalism. Ironically, given our area of work, this meant participating in behaviour that would get you kicked out of almost any other place of business. Fans don't want to witness a group of males drinking green juice who appear to be on their way to the library. They want to witness wild, unrestrained, virile maniacs. You must be doing everything they wish they could do. We were fairly good at filling those roles. It was our job to be animals.

Dave, in particular, was into physical achievements at that stage in his life. He started working out with the LA Lakers' trainer. He went climbing in New Guinea's Star Mountains with these guides known as the Jungle Studs (which can be both hilarious and tragic depending on your attitude). When we were in Italy promoting the album, Dave was practising his jumps from the drum riser for a picture shoot when he hit his nose on a low-hanging disco ball. (Yes, I am serious.) The European press loved his bandaged-up nose, and Dave enjoyed the spotlight so much that I believe he broke his nose a second time spinning the mic stand years later, when we were performing on Jimmy Kimmel Live, just to garner more attention! Dave is an entertainment personality.

More European medical weirdness: for reasons I don't understand, our French distributors had us shoot a promotional video for the song "Loss of Control" in an operating room. You have to give them credit: there was no MTV or VH1, so they were not just following the crowd, but leading it. You can check it up online, and oh, that video is bizarre. It begins with Dave lying on the stage, wailing, with a beautiful nurse on top of him. But it doesn't look sexy; rather, it appears that she was hit with a tranquiliser dart and collapsed on top of him, smiling bizarrely while he cries. Then he gets up and dances in a doctor's coat over his striped spandex and suspenders, while the rest of us play in scrubs and I have X-ray film taped to my drums.

His need for publicity caused a quandary. On the one hand, this is excellent. We dislike talking, and because Dave enjoys it so much, we rarely have to. (And there was a constant demand: once you start playing the fame game rather than just producing music, momentum builds, and before you know it, you're committing all of your time and energy to feeding the machine. Do you want to be on the cover of the magazine? You need to do the interview and disclose your guts. No thanks; we're trying to operate a band here, which is a full-time job! The problem is that we can't always let Dave do things on his own. You can't have just one person out there representing Van Halen and giving the notion that he is the band. When Peter Grant managed Led Zeppelin, he was always very clear about publicity: you either get them all or none of them. That's the brand, and that's the band. So, there's the conundrum.

You must be a cohesive organism, both in the public's eyes and in reality! Because a band is a fragile equilibrium. And this is visible in who gets which accommodation, which part of the bus, and so on. People begin to act strangely in terms of the social hierarchy. There is a lot of jockeying for territory, whether it's creative territory, who gets to choose the order of the songs on the record, or who gets the first burger and has to wait two minutes longer for his to arrive. Every day on tour, there are a million little possibilities to be disappointed and feel slighted. There are a million ways to be a jerk and make a big deal out of something that you should simply ignore.

By the same token, Ed has every magazine and artist telling him he's the best guitarist to ever live. And he says he's just a vessel, and he seems humble, but that message, combined with a lot of coke, starts to play with his head. He is less willing to tolerate Dave's insane behaviour. When Ted objects to any outrageous proposal, he loses his sense of humour. Or, put another way, you begin to trust your own lies. You lose sight of the idea that, while you may be the soup of the day, in the grand scheme of things, you are still just a speck.

Chapter 12

Valerie Bertinelli heard our music for the first time after borrowing our records from her brothers. She was only nineteen years old, but she was already well-known for her role as Barbara Cooper in the Norman Lear sitcom One Day at a Time. And she was the sole provider for her entire family. That's a lot of pressure and power for a youngster, which is exactly what Valerie was when the Bertinellis relocated to Los Angeles to pursue her television career. That summer, she arrived backstage at our gig in Shreveport, her hometown, with a brother or two and a gift for the band: a bag of M&Ms. (Note to the wise: August is not the best month to visit Louisiana. (It was hot.)

Dave didn't like it right away—there was this new famous atmosphere around that had nothing to do with him. Here's how he describes their first encounter: "One of the front office guys walks in and says, 'Dave, this is Valerie Bertinelli.'" I didn't know who she was. "I had absolutely no interest." You get the idea. He had a bad attitude about her from the beginning. Remember, celebrity was the entire objective for him. Valerie had a large audience back then, and everyone knew who she was. So she was taking up part of the attention in the Van Halen orbit, which drove Dave insane.

When we first started performing in clubs, hard rock was out of trend; it was the singer-songwriter era. Look at the late-70s Rolling Stone covers: Bruce Springsteen, Carly Simon, Linda Ronstadt, James Taylor, and Jackson Browne. You take a blender, add the antiwar movement, a pair of moccasins, a lot of long brown hair, an acoustic guitar, and a load of major seventh chords, and voila, you've got yourself the easy-drinking milkshake that is the singer-songwriter. Blink, and the pendulum has swung fully the other way, from these soulful, innocuous crooners to the plastic pop of the Go-Go's, the Cars, and Devo—also a bunch of pleasant white people, but with skinny ties and synthesisers. We certainly did not fit in with any of this or anything else going on at the time, including disco, punk, folk, and funk. I am starting to sound like Dr. Seuss.

People replicated both Ed's guitars and his playing style. Charvel, a company he had admired, began offering a duplicate of Ed's guitar: a Strat-style body with a humbucker and tremolo. He had to file a lawsuit to get them to stop. Then a man asked whether he could use Ed's name to promote a unique pickup he intended to manufacture. Ed said no way. "Next time I pick up Guitar Player magazine there's a special Van Halen model," Ed said with irritation. We eventually ceased that as well. But kids couldn't stop themselves from duplicating Ed's stripes and painting them on their guitars—they were everywhere.

However, those bands did not meet our musical criteria. For us, hair and makeup, outrageous outfits, and a spectacular show with things bursting into flames were just the frosting on the cake. That was the full piece of pastry for most hair metal bands in the 1980s. Well, as Dave used to say, Van Halen can play with nothing but a bare lightbulb and still kick your ass.

Our fourth album was tougher and less cheerful than the ones that came before it. It's a tougher rock, and it may serve as a warning—or at least a challenge—to our imitators. It was, as the title suggests, a Fair Warning: It doesn't matter whether you had long hair, leather leggings, and an androgynous blond front man. There's just one Van Halen. I came across this painting of a man pushing against a brick wall with his head by Canadian-Ukrainian artist William Kurelek, which I wanted to incorporate on the record jacket. Kurelek was like us: an immigrant who arrived in Canada without knowing a word of English and had to adjust. He was a cultural outsider who possessed a knack, in this case visual art. If the devastation of WWII and its toll on our elderly father moulded our viewpoint, Kurelek's reference point was the savagery of World War I. His paintings were a reaction to that history—and to the ferocious aspect of human nature i general.

Kurelek's image of that man, ramming his head against the wal conveyed to me the sense of battle that comes with being alive—anc of course, being in a band. No matter how hard you battle for you point of view, being a member of a group forces you to make regula concessions, which you frequently despise. Around that time, E informed a Creem interviewer that he was doing exactly what h wanted. When people ask if I want to record a solo album, I answer 'What the fuck for?' Playing with Van Halen is like recording a sol album. Complete freedom to do whatever I want." This is complet BS! In a band, there is no such thing. You never stop making concessions, big and small. That is the price of collaboration.

It all came to a head while we were recording "Unchained" (Ed fel shackled, ironically). "Ted didn't like what Ed was playing and E did not want to play what Ted was suggesting," Donn pointed out "That whole day, making that whole song go together, was crisi after crisis—I've never had a day like that working with anyon before. Ted tortured Ed, and he still had no idea.

Ted knew Ed was never entirely unrestrained when he was present "There wasn't a better guitarist walking the earth in 1981 than E Van Halen, but I could tell that he'd sometimes get nervous aroun me when we were working in the studio," Ted writes in his memoir "When I was gone, he loosened up." But it was larger than that. E was at conflict with Ted because he believed he knew more abou music than any producer—which was true—and he desired th flexibility to attempt new things. To hear Ted tell it, he was tryin his hardest to accommodate Ed: "Occasionally, when he was tryin to push the envelope, I couldn't decode and translate what he wa after," Ted added. "I don't think Ed realised how irritated I was whe he tried to describe a sound or sensation to me and I couldn't do it fo him. I've always wanted to make him happy.

This was also an issue with Dave. We'd always been on opposite sides of the musical spectrum in terms of taste, but it was becoming increasingly difficult to find the crossover, the style that merged his flamboyant craziness with our sound. Don't get me wrong, we still made it; Fair Warning is a terrific record in my opinion. Or Ted, for that matter: "There were other heavy metal bands who combined monster riffs with outstanding lyrics. However, none of them could compete with Van Halen's songwriting and sense of humour. The breakdown of 'Unchained' demonstrates what set Van Halen apart from their competition." Even though we didn't have a big pop hit to feed the system, we still had our third platinum record, Fair Warning, which peaked at number five on the Billboard chart, marking a new high for us.

Now, were Ed and Valerie the happy couple, America's sweethearts, that they were portrayed as? Listen, they had no idea what they were doing; they were kids. Though not as young as my father thought, when he first learned about Ed's new girlfriend, he watched One Day at a Time to get a feel for her. Then he called Ed and said no way; he was completely opposed to Ed marrying a fifteen-year-old. Ed had to explain to his father that he had been watching reruns. They got engaged four months after meeting, on New Year's Eve 1980. They began planning a large Hollywood wedding with four or five hundred guests before they even knew each other. Hell, at that age, they barely knew who they were!

It's hard to argue with that. But they stayed together for 25 years, so they must have done something well. We married on April 11, 1981, just before the premiere of Fair Warning. My mother was pleased that the ceremony took place at Saint Paul's Catholic Church. Ed was going to be married, with a Catholic woman, and he was going to wear a suit! So, a white tuxedo. Close enough.

This is from a review of our sold-out event in Manhattan in July 1981 by the famed critic Stephen Holden of the New York Times:

"The music that is keeping the record business afloat is the heavy metal brand of hard rock established by Led Zeppelin in the late 1960s." And the triumphal appearance of Van Halen, one of the heaviest of heavy metal rock bands, at Madison Square Garden on Friday was impressive evidence." Personally, I do not consider Van Halen to be heavy metal. But, clearly, I adore it when people refer to us as the American Zeppelin, in so many words. That is a comparison I will accept any day of the week. Holden added that Ed "wielded his guitar like a lethal weapon."

When Ed married, he moved out of our parents' house before I did. I chose to stay in Pasadena and keep my father company—it was evident that someone other than our mother needed to do so or he wouldn't be around for long. He was quite bored. My mother disliked being alone at night, so she stopped him from going out to play. Dad was basically falling apart and drinking excessively, which was unusual for him. I was attempting to keep him entertained; without music, marriage was insufficient. Not long after Ed, Mikey married Sue, his high school love. In any case, they were effectively wedded. Aside from his love of Jack Daniel's, Mike was a very good man. While we were buying automobiles, he was collecting Mickey Mouse paraphernalia. Van Halen played his wedding.

I tried it, too. After Ed's wedding, I married a girl I had been dating for a few years. (For a while, we had a second girl staying with us. What was it like? Busy.) Two months after the wedding, we were already planning the divorce. So I got married again a year later. Do you remember what Oscar Wilde said about second marriages? The triumph of optimism over experience. Third time's a charm. I'm not going to discuss the first two experiments because I don't think they count. I was practising for Stone.

Music led me to her. Stine worked as an art director at Warner Bros. in the mid-1990s. At the time, I was the band's point man for such activities. The first time I came into her office, everything was clean and basic, with the exception of an orange beanbag and a green pickle jar on her desk. The contrast between those two colours was stunning, and it reflected Stine's vibrancy as a person. Design for her was more than simply a job; it was a means of communication. She chose those two artefacts because of the impact juxtaposition would have on the observer. In this case, it's me. And I was dazzled.

Stine was born in Copenhagen, where I live, and comes from a family of artistic Jewish individualists. Talking to her that day made me feel at home. She knew what I was saying. We shared a way of seeing the world. The same things made us giggle. Then there was the miniskirt. Everything was simple and fascinating at the same time. I owe that woman my life. She loved me enough—and had the strength—to say, "I'm out of here," when she saw me falling into addiction. I can still picture her coming out the door, carrying our pet in a box. I became addicted to benzos while on tour in 1995. I wasn't sleeping since I was in a lot of discomfort. I have a spinal injury from that boat accident with Gregg in the 1970s, and it got to the point where certain movements would cause me to be temporarily paralyzed. My neck was killing me, and without sleep, my body was disintegrating. The tour manager offered me two Valiums, which was amazing. Wow. It was the first time I had slept in months! The relief was great.

Everyone on the business end of things was calling me, advising me what to do and how I should go about quitting the pills. But it was evident that they were not attempting to save me; they were trying to save their own money. The show must go on so that everyone can be paid, and they needed me back on the road. None of this helped. Stine had lost her brother, a renowned jazz drummer, to a heroin overdose. She understood the nature of addiction and the only way to communicate with an addict. (Her brother, according to Stone, was similar to Ed: a prodigy who was given an exceptional ability but battled greatly to function in the real world—the hard stuff was easy for him, but the easy stuff was difficult.) The only price I refused to pay for the medicine was Stine's death.

Once I've decided on anything, there's no stopping me. So Stine moved back in with Emma, a wild cat from downtown Los Angeles. We had hell for four or five weeks while I was coming off the drugs, hallucinating, screaming, travelling to another dimension... and then being extremely concerned that I'd left my shoes there, which I was convinced would cause havoc, because obviously, changing something in another dimension can have disastrous consequences in your own dimension. I had become sober in 1987, and I thought it was difficult. But quitting benzos was far more difficult than quitting alcohol. When you are going through withdrawal, all of the knowledge that has ever entered your brain becomes entirely confused. But you are not aware of this! It is not like taking acid and expecting to have hallucinations. This gradually creeps up on you, and you believe it's true. I was hearing the same music over and over in my head—Zeppelin, of course; I can't remember which one—and it was driving me insane. It wouldn't stop, day after day. I eventually discovered a means to shield myself—from fame, the music industry, drugs, and booze. With Stine, I was able to create a home apart from my job and celebrity.

Chapter 13

Neuroscientists discuss convergent and divergent thinking, two types of thinking that lead to creativity. Divergent thinking is about looking for uniqueness, letting your mind go wild in the hopes of arriving somewhere fresh. Brainstorming. You toss out a lot of stuff and see what sticks to the wall; you are open to the directions your mind takes. You can arrive at far-fetched concepts in that state that appear unrelated to one another, shooting all over the place and overlapping like the lines on Ed's guitar. He had an aptitude for this type of thinking. And I had a talent for backing him up, both rhythmically and emotionally. Together, we were productive. We created music out of thin air.

The creative process, of course, necessitates convergent thinking, which means synthesising, absorbing, and assimilating a plethora of ideas and inspirations. Dave was good at it. Some fans created a documentary on us, and they interviewed one of Dave's good friends from school, who said it best: "You have to get it from somewhere... and if you don't have it within, you have to get it from whatever is around you." Dave drew inspiration from a variety of sources, including cartoons, books, movies, and musicals, and added his own unique spin on them. We often encouraged him to do anything he wanted and laughed at his wacky ideas because we wanted all of him—his entire soul. I did not just want him to be the clown!

We realised that his energy created a contrapuntal force that offset what Ed and I did, similar to how two colours on opposite ends of the spectrum highlight each other. When you put orange next to green, both hues yell at you, which is kind of exhilarating. And if you locate just the right shade of each, you'll have something both elegant and interesting—a contrast with sophistication. That's what we were looking for.

But I believe (and know) Dave was upset with Ed for being so talented. I believe he sold himself short by competing with Ec Simply appreciate your own gift! We do! The bottom line is tha Dave wanted to be an artist, but something was always missing. H could never truly feel the music; it was all cerebral. He missed th part where you need to connect with something deeper, such as th eternal force of the universe. That's how you create art. Yo eliminate your ego and attempt to turn off the thinking, calculatin part of your brain. You can't plan on touching a dragon's tail.

You want to get it back; it's annoying and terrible when it escape you. So you strive to recreate the precise conditions that existe when the magic happened. You eat the same meal, wear your righ shoe before your left, and snort the same number of lines. Musician are often superstitious, and we were raised by a mother from th islands, which are the most superstitious people on the earth. (W were never meant to leave a glass fully empty, for example—Mon instructed us to always put something in there to keep thing balanced.) You can spend your entire life attempting to repeat wha occurred before. I truly feel that is what cost my brother his life.

Drugs and alcohol were prevalent during our early rise t prominence in American consciousness. So returning to then repeatedly was part of an attempt to revert to the original formula Just the perfect degree of intoxication can open "the doors o perception," as Aldous Huxley put it. Huxley talked on how the brai filters the immense amounts of stimuli that enter every second of th day via our eyes, hands, mouths, noses, and, most importantly, ears At any given time, we are bombarded with so much information tha if we didn't filter part of it out, we'd never get anything done an would definitely go insane. Huxley referred to this as a "reducing valve" that blurs out what we don't need.

However, in order to create music or art, you must periodically (often) turn off the reducing valve and let everything flow. You neec to feel and hear everything. You require a different level of access tc your own senses and sensitivities. So, how do you obtain that? You take in whatever you can find, whatever works for you, to change your consciousness.

What you need to do is let your mind go. When you take drugs, you lose a vital component of your brain. Stop thinking, "I can't do that because it has never been done." All of that goes out the window. It makes no difference if someone else says, "Don't even bother with that," It is irrelevant. Because now you can simply go with the flow. That explains why so many creative people experiment with drugs. You have to tune out the voices that prevent you from exploring and simply enjoy your craft. ("Are you experienced?" Have you ever experienced this? "Well, I have." There's a reason he named it the Jimi Hendrix Experience.

BY THE END OF '81, we'd spent four years on the road or in the studio. We were exhausted after the Fair Warning tour; none of us wanted to make another record right immediately. We wanted to catch our breath. And Ed was a newlywed! So, to slow things down without fully disappearing, we decided to begin 1982 by releasing a single rather than a new album.

We debuted our video in early 1982. Within weeks, it was prohibited. First in Japan, then in Australia. It upset their delicate sensibilities, and we were not allowed on the airwaves. That's bad news, right? Not for us. The whole affair got a lot of attention, and we're no longer just the men who play loud music, have drunken food fights, and despise brown M&Ms; we're also victims of censorship! We are supporters of free expression! I adore America.

Our version of "Pretty Woman" began to ascend the charts. Isn't this good news? Not for us. Because now that we've got a smash, Warner Bros. wants to capitalise on it. And in order for that to happen, they need a record to sell quickly, before the song is no longer on the radio. They asked that we record one quickly to follow the song.

"We're going wait a minute, we just did that to keep us out there, so people knew we were still alive," Ed said to Jas Obrecht during a 1982 interview, "but they just kept pressuring, 'We need that album, we need that album,' so we jumped right back in, without any rest, without any time to recuperate from the tour, and started recording." Instead of interrupting the annual cycle of recording and touring, we managed to speed it up.

This is what I am talking about. Ed created the chord progression for "Jump"—our biggest hit, our lone number one single, an anthem that has become legendary all over the world and will most likely survive anything else we did—in 1982. (It originated from the intro to "Hear About It Later," a song Ed wrote for Fair Warning—it's basically the same chord progression and concept, but sped up and rearranged.) Ed played it for everyone, trying to get it on Diver Down. Dave thought it was lame.

So there was all this friction. On top of that, we were all discouraged and fatigued; we had no desire to embark on a tour, and new covers were the last thing we wanted to release. "I hated every minute of making it," Ed admitted of Diver Down. "Come on, Van Halen performing 'Dancing in the Street'? It was dumb. I started feeling like I'd rather fail playing my own tunes than succeed with someone else's." For the album jacket, we chose the red and white flag that goes up to indicate that divers are diving deep beneath the surface: a recycled image for a record of recycled tunes.

On the back cover of Diver Down, we used a photo I've long loved of the four of us onstage bidding farewell to a sea of people at the end of a show. Take a look: a large audience, right? Yes, because it's a Stones audience! HA! It began in the afternoon of October 1981, when we opened for the Rolling Stones in Orlando. Yet another example of our marketing brilliance. (Obviously, we got permission from them to use it, and we gave it our all for that crowd, as you can see in the photo.)

Don't you know it: Diver Down out-sold Fair Warning. Did well on the charts, peaking at number three. Because of Dave's influence, half of the tracks did not feature guitar solos for the first time. Ed was so furious about it all—disagreements with Ted about "Unchained," fights with Dave over, well, everything—that he wanted to break up the band. We used to get into fistfights about it backstage. "Are you crazy?" I told him. "After all the work we've done to get here?" I assumed that throwing everything away would be a huge mistake, and that Dave would walk away with all of the marbles.

Diver Down had one undeniable highlight: we were able to get our father to play. Dave had the notion to cover "Big Bad Bill (Is Sweet William Now)." He had a Walkman, and you could record on it if you heard something interesting while listening to the radio. "If he pointed the antenna in a specific direction in his room, he'd pick up this strange... "I'm not sure what you'd call that type of music," Ed told Jas Obrecht. "He played it for us, and we simply laughed ourselves stupid. I'm like, "This is bad!" "Let's do it!" It was such an odd style of music for us—we all laughed at how strange it would be to have a 1930s quintet on a Van Halen album. It was also Dave's suggestion to have our father play clarinet on that song. Dave's goals might have been strategic, but I don't care what drove him. I'll be forever grateful to Dave for coming up with that. The outcome was extremely cool.

My father was past his prime and eager to get out of the house. This was an excellent opportunity for him to become involved in the band's existence and, of course, its music. It was an extremely humbling experience to record with him. He was becoming increasingly anxious, and it was now our turn to guide him through a professional experience. We'd spent our entire lives looking up to him, asking him to explain how things worked when it came to playing... everything!

My father's nose had changed colour as a result of the booze. We could have enrolled him in an AA program if we had known about it at the time, but we had no idea about the twelve steps. He was crumbling and declining in front of our eyes. After Dad suffered a heart attack in 1986, he told me, "Alex, I don't want to be here anymore." I wanted to deck him, to be honest. You don't get to die yet; you're just sixty-six! I still need you around. As far as I'm concerned, becoming a father means giving up your right to die young. There have been occasions when I wanted to leave stage left because I was in so much pain, but I have two sons and I'm not going away by choice. You bring another person into this world; I believe the least you can do is be with them for as long as possible.

However, my father was in horrible shape. A lifetime of drinking had damaged his physique and was having a negative impact on his mentality. His organs started failing, and he died a few months later. Dad received his wish. I was devastated. We walked into the studio, Mikey was there, and we played for four or five hours straight. It was all we knew to do to deal with our pain. I completely fell apart. Alcohol became more dangerous and confusing than ever for me. On the one hand, I'm sad, and perhaps even angry, that my father drank himself to death. Alcohol suddenly reveals itself as a poison, capable of killing you, your father, and ruining your life. On the other hand, drinking is something my father and I did together. I miss the person, I'll never see him again, and this is how we communicated.

Chapter 14

So, based on the remark above, Ed came up with the idea that when you're in a band, you should put everything you've got into it. It will never work if you spread your energies in a dozen different directions. For a band to succeed, everyone in it must be focused on moving the entity forward as a collective mission. That is how we got to where we are. But then, in '82, Ed received a call from Quincy Jones asking him to play on Michael Jackson's song, and everything changed. He asked if I felt he should do it, and I replied, "No! Use your head: they want you to extend Jackson's appeal. If you want to extend our appeal, Jackson should be on the record! It is not in Van Halen's best interests for you to perform with other acts.

"Beat It" became number one all around the world. Ed's cameo on Thriller became one of the most iconic solos in rock history, although it was not on a Van Halen album. It wasn't simply a solo, either; Ed had completely changed the track. ("I listened to the song and immediately said, 'Can I change some parts?'" I turned to the engineer and said, 'Okay, from the breakdown, chop this portion, go to this piece, pre-chorus, chorus, out.' It took him about ten minutes to put it together. Ed revealed on air that he proceeded to improvise two solos over it. Ed's musical contribution to "Beat It" was fairly extensive.

Around the same time, ED worked on another side project that was far less obvious than playing on Thriller, yet it proved to be just as important. He'd become friends with Frank Zappa, who lived nearby in Coldwater Canyon, where Ed had moved in with Valerie. Ed also got to know Frank's twelve-year-old son Dweezil over there, and he was quite nice to him. Ed gave Dweezil one of his own guitars and taught him some tunes on it. ("Of course I asked Edward to play 'Mean Street' and 'Eruption,'" Dweezil replied.) "I got to see it up close. "The techniques he used were burned into my brain forever.")

But get this: Ed and Donna agreed to produce Dweezil's firs single—the child is in junior high! I'm not sure what possessed them

After a few weeks at Zappa's, Ed was determined that the only wa to achieve true freedom was to create his own studio in Coldwate Canyon. And now that he was married to a very affluent networ television star, it was totally possible. (A side note regarding thei mansion and wealth: Around the time they married, my mother cam over to see where her son would be living. Valerie has a larg collection of antiques. After our mother left, she called Ed and askec "Can't you afford some new furniture?" "I can lend you the money. Valerie was interested in creating a studio. We were on the road s much, I'm sure she appreciated the concept that when Ed came home he could actually be at home rather than at Sunset Sound or Amig Studios. Ed and Valerie took turns on a Caterpillar, tearing down portion of the old guesthouse to make place for us.

Drew, one of the Nellies, had been living there with his partner fo quite some time. He was in construction, so we decided to give hin the task of building the studio to compensate for the fact that we ha commandeered his home. Donn planned it, and Drew built i alongside this man Ron Fry, who came up with an excellent solutio to our toughest challenge. You couldn't secure a permit to develop studio on your residential property. But Ron responded, "Hey, studio cannot have windows; it must be soundproof." Let's seek permit for a racquetball court and then remodel it. (The authoritie did not hesitate to issue permits for racquetball courts. It was th 1980s, and every celebrity was building one of those blasted things So they acquired the permit, built the court, and we playe racquetball for about three weeks. The court's concrete walls wer thick enough to keep out any sound bleed from the 50,000-watt radi tower a few miles away. Ed was always skilled at retrofittin things—guitars, cars—so it seemed right that he would have a studi that started out as something else.

One day, his friend Steve Lukather, the guitarist from Toto, stopped by to visit the home. Ed is giving him a tour: this is the control room, this is the studio, and this is where I keep my gun! Ed had a new .44 Magnum—which, if you know anything about weapons, is a completely absurd choice for self-defence; it's like a cannon. Ed was used to a Colt, but this was a Smith & Wesson, and the cylinder turns in the opposite direction, so when he looked at the cylinder and saw no bullets, he concluded it wasn't loaded. Long story short, KABOOM. Ed shot a hole right through the concrete wall, and the bullet exited the opposite side. Donn came up with the appropriate name for the location: 5150. It is the police code for involuntary imprisonment of a mentally ill patient who poses a threat to himself or the community. (Donn was living in Malibu at the time and was always listening to his scanner to keep track of the wildfires in the mountains, so he learned all of the police codes.) Everyone said we were insane for building a studio when we had world-class facilities in Los Angeles. Calling it 5150 was our way of claiming the room as our own private mad institution.

Once 5150 was up and running, we began working all hours of the day and night. It was fun there! The atmosphere was laid-back, and we didn't keep time. Most nights, I'd stay there until three a.m., and Donn and Ed would often continue after I left. (Remember, I was the one who didn't drink Coke!) Nobody there told us that keyboards were a horrible idea or that Van Halen was intended to be heavy metal. It was quite liberating, similar to how we used to experiment and jam in our childhood bands.

Ed and Donn had become good friends, but the three of us got along wonderfully and had a real mind meld going on. We had the time and space to do any odd thing we wanted: Donn placed small microphones all around Ed's Lamborghini, for example, since we thought we may utilise the sound of the engine idling—it ended up on "Panama." Then there was "Stereo Septic": Drew Bertinelli had left all kinds of trash in the guesthouse that we wanted to get rid of, and immediately next to us on the property was a large pit that used to hold the septic tank before they switched to using the sewage system. We wondered, "Hmm, what can we fit in there?" And one day, we dropped all of Drew's debris into the pit, and Donn documented it. I recall the Electrolux vacuum dying slowly and producing some fantastic sounds along the way.

But it irritated Ed—and both of us—to be instructed not to evolve as artists, not to experiment with new instruments and ideas. Remember how we grew up? My father told us that we could make music on a chair! It's fun to innovate and create. If you're fortunate enough to have a concept for something different from what you've previously done? You get it! Jesus, that is the entire point of what we do! This isn't Gazzarri's; we're not going to become a four-man jukebox playing exclusively Van Halen's "songs of the seventies."

We didn't see it as "going pop." Ed had been listening to a lot of classical music when he came up with the "Jump" riff. Listen, what I consider to be mainstream music may be heavy metal for you. All of these categories are marketing jargon rather than meaningful descriptors. I will say it again: it is music. If something sounds good, it probably is. That's what we set out to do: create something exceptional. And I believe we achieved that in 1984. It's the album that got closest to the sound we were always looking for, and it's still the record I'm most proud of and like listening to. The same was true for Ed.

Getting Dave on board was a huge pain in the ass—"It was like pulling teeth to get him to sing the damn song," Ed said. But I have to give it to Dave: when did he finally stop complaining and write the lyrics? He did an excellent job. (Initially, Ted was afraid that Dave was creating a song inciting suicide: "You want to kill yourself, sucker?" Go ahead and jump. According to Ted, Dave told him, "No, no, no!" That is not what I meant, Teddy. I mean, you need to find your nerve. Take a chance. Ask that beautiful girl across the room to dance, even if she says no. You're concerned that she'll reject you, but life is all about taking a chance and jumping!" It's difficult to argue with that. His lyrics were a wonderful match for the chords and sound. Uplifting. Anthemic. "I get up and nothing' gets me down / You got it tough, I've seen the toughest around / And I know, baby, just how you feel / You got to roll with the punches to get to what's real." Soon, we'd hear tens of thousands of supporters yelling those words back at us.

ALL OF OUR OTHER ALBUMS WERE MADE IN A WEEK OR TWO. 1984 lasted over a year. There were interruptions: we went to play the US Festival—and were paid a million and a half dollars to do so! (It felt like an insane amount of money at the time; it was completely unheard of. We hoped it marked the start of a new era in which Van Halen made money for himself rather than for others. Then we had to take a pause so Ed could record the music for one of Valerie's TV shows, which none of us were excited about. The major reason we took so long to make that record was because we could.

At the time, we considered work to be fun. Being really fatigued and still coming up with something fantastic... it's a nice time. What was the motive to stop? "And we could always collapse on the floor," Donn jokes. "We did this several times. Wake up and ask yourself, "Where were we last night?" Oh, right. Here.' We just wanted each song to be the best it could possibly be." 5150 felt like our own tiny kingdom, where we created all the rules. What else does a twenty something guy want? What else would anyone want?

Dave was becoming increasingly agitated. He wasn't going to stay up all night there—not that he was especially welcome. There were periods during the day when Ed needed to crash and Dave wanted to work. He was used to acting as if it was his band, but now that Ed was in command of the recording, he couldn't pretend.

Ed controlled the studio, so we could control the mix as well, and finally—finally!—get the heaviness we'd always desired, that thunderous, Zeppelin-like massiveness of sound. It's difficult to put into words what we were looking for; if you could put sound into words, you wouldn't need it! But Ed and I were always thinking about the same thing: music that sounds "like Godzilla waking up," as Ed put it. Donn now comprehended our aim. We would not have had 1984 if Donn hadn't been adaptable and willing to listen, experiment, and do things differently.

Unfortunately, Ted could not stand the sound we adored—the brown sound we finally attained in 1984. ("I complained about how loud the drums were. But Al insisted on increasing the volume of the drums in the mix, and Donn and Ed agreed," Ted protested. "When we mixed, those three guys became of one mind.") He had different tastes, and that is understandable. I'm not even claiming he had awful taste—take a look at all the excellent albums created by Ted Templeman! I completely realise that Ted has twenty bands to manage and twenty different new albums to release at any given time, which is not simple. But we just have one band, and it is our entire existence.

This is our voice. If Ed had to construct a studio to record it, if we had to sneak around with Donn, if we had to defy Ted and Dave, whatever it took, we were going to make an album that sounded like us. THE PROOF IS IN THE RESULTS. 1984 sold more than ten million copies. Rolling Stone described it as "the album that brings all of Van Halen's talent into focus." The song "Jump" received three Grammy nominations. Ted apparently admitted to Donn that 1984 was to Van Halen what Sgt. Pepper was to the Beatles: a full flowering of the band's brilliance. The work of musicians who had a mature grasp of their goals and were determined not to give up until they attained them.

Chapter 15

A Rolling Stone writer attended our sold-out tour in early 1984, and something leaps out to me now when I reread the story "Van Halen's Split Personality." I believe my brother took my (first) divorce after two months of marriage harder than I did! "If I could suck the pain out of Alex, I would," Ed told the reporter before crying! "There are too many people on this basketball that's floating around the sun who are too afraid to allow themselves to feel," according to him. "... Hey, goddamnit, I can cry, be hot, laugh, anything I want. I'm not capable of holding things in." Yeah, Ed—especially after a bottle of Blue Nun!

I'll repeat it: he was sensitive. Drunk or sober, joyful or depressed, the world simply got to him. Ed conveyed all of that passion through his song, grin, and tears. Life had just taken him by storm. After 1984, the conflict with Ted and Dave exhausted him. (Apparently, my divorce did not help, either! HA!) Ed just wanted the conflict to end.

And it happened quickly, following our greatest tour, for our best record, and supporting our only number one single.

It all started when Dave announced that he was planning to release a solo EP, which Ted would produce. After all the criticism you gave Ed about "Beat It" and his guitar solos in general, you're going to make your own record?! You cannot be serious, Dave! Everything felt ridiculous, ludicrous. (And speaking of ludicrous, Dave's musical taste went to hell in a handbasket without us to reel him in, in my opinion.)

The next thing we know, he has written a screenplay. He called it "Crazy from the Heat." He gave his EP and memoir the same name, and he couldn't get enough of the title. What is it about? DAVE!! A rock star named David Lee Roth travels to the Dongo Islands with his entourage of freaks for wild tropical exploits. Want to watch two-hour version of his "California Girls" video? This is it! He ha the guts to inform Ed that he would let us score it. That was their las conversation for a time.

It was arrogance. He believed that we were holding him back despite the fact that we were all propelling each other forward. W were more than the sum of our parts.

Rage is always with me, and I had plenty of it as Dave was leavin, the band... little by little, until one day... Holy crap, did that clow just quit?! It's like Hemingway's comment about how to go bankrup "There are two ways. "Gradually, then suddenly." That marked th end of the original Van Halen.

I was upset, but also perplexed: we're at the pinnacle of our careers things are now reaching the level we've hoped for since we wer kids, and you want to change the formula right now? Do you realis how lucky we are, Dave? How unusual is this? We finally sound lik ourselves!

"What are you thinking????""When I left Van Halen, it wasn something I was looking forward to doing," Dave admitted a doze years later. "I wasn't celebrating. I wasn't relieved. It was one of th scariest times of my life." Hindsight is 20/20. Dave had recentl signed a film deal with CBS, and he was confident that his future a a writer/director/actor would make his debut in the music industr look mundane in contrast. Then the movie agreement fell through And he never received another one.

I am not gloating. I don't enjoy admitting that we were all bette together, no matter how often we argued or how annoyed I an thinking about it. ""When Dave left the band, Alex, Mike, and I wer just devastated," Ed remarked a few years later, after the rage hac subsided. "We were simply sitting there going, 'Now what? We'v worked with this person for eleven years, and he just went away."

The entire purpose of a band is that you're in it together: blood in, blood out. You've agreed that the only way you'll leave is in a pine box. That's why we told Ted to fuck off from the start when he asked us to replace our singer. That's why I convinced Ed to stay when he wanted to leave in 1982. Dave's departure after the people voted in our favour as a group seemed like treason. Like extremely foolish treason. "Example of premature evacuation!""Everyone in the band felt let down," Dave wrote. "Everyone in the band felt abandoned." I felt exactly what they were feeling. Two opposites become the same thing. 'Oh, Dave was working on something else.' "No, that is what Ed was doing." It's easy to see what's wrong with the other guy. It is much more difficult to recognize your own mistakes. Marriage is simple compared to keeping four grown men together year after year of relentless touring, performing, marketing, and recording. Especially because one of them is your younger brother and the other is an egomaniac!

On the one hand, we were relieved Dave was gone since he was so far up his own ass. However, there is a sense that something is wrong with the artwork.

Something isn't right.

We have had many different singers over the years. We enjoyed more success later, when we finally got the manager we deserved, Ed Leffler. (Another guy I miss. He couldn't have been a greater friend to us, a better employee, or a better person overall. (See you on the other side, Leffler.)

However, creativity is a contentious issue among friends. And we've never fought better than we did with Dave.

It was as if we threw all of our ideas into a dogfight, and whomever made it out alive made it on stage. "If that conflict gnawed away at all of us constantly, out of it came earthshaking, culture-changing music," Dave observed. He's correct; it's undeniable.

After Ed died, Dave was the first person I called and wanted to speak with. Just out of mutual respect for what we accomplished with my brother, with whom none of us would ever work again in our lifetime.

THE TWO EVENTS ARE NOT OF THE SAME SIZE, but the sensations I had when Dave bailed—of unfairness, rage, loss, and perplexity about the workings of the universe—were like a foreshadowing of the huge anguish that overtook me after my brother died. And there was the familiar sense of a horrible outcome occurring both gradually and unexpectedly. Don't get me wrong, there is no comparable. (The first thing is a paper cut. The second is having your head chopped off.) After Dave left Van Halen, we went on; it wasn't the end of the world or the band. In terms of my brother, it took me almost a year to write this book, and he died about four years ago. I still wake up most mornings thinking, Ed! Where the fuck you are? I will never get over it. I will never say goodbye.

I've been thinking a lot about the beginning lately. In some ways, the distant past seems more vivid than what occurred last week! I had dreams of the boat voyage from Holland, playing piano in the banquet hall with the scent of the boat, and hoping to meet that dark-haired little girl. Pasadena, California—the Promised Land! Those phrases and sounds are so completely absent from Dutch. And the hues! My uncle's baby-blue Ford: oranges for a penny. The Broken Combs. My mother, with her purse full of meat. Throwing a bottle at Red Ball Jet. The stabbing in Walter Mitty's. Electric Lady and Gene. Sprinting off the Ventura Freeway in platform shoes to our major meeting at Warner Bros. That night in Scotland, we discovered we had gone gold! My relative grabbed gold records from Las Lunas Street. Looking for Ozzy in the stairwells and watching him shoot those duck decoys out of his pond. Castaic Lake with Gregg, Ed, and my old father, all of whom were alive that day but are no longer. Ed's wedding—the most inebriated I've ever seen him. The first time he played me a riff from "Jump." That night, in Nuremberg, Germany, we performed our final gig as the original Van Halen.

"We sold the idea of imagination," says Dave, "extreme imagination, forced to the breaking point." And we broke. It was the most disappointing experience I'd ever had, and it seemed the most wasteful and unjust.

Until I lost my brother.

Made in United States
North Haven, CT
11 December 2024

62059439R00055